Classical Music
A Beginner's Guide

ONEWORLD BEGINNER'S GUIDES combine an original, inventive, and engaging approach with expert analysis on subjects ranging from art and history to religion and politics, and everything in between. Innovative and affordable, books in the series are perfect for anyone curious about the way the world works and the big ideas of our time.

Beginners
GUIDES

Classical Music
A Beginner's Guide

Julian Johnson

ONEWORLD

OXFORD

A Oneworld Paperback Original

Published by Oneworld Publications 2009

Copyright © Julian Johnson 2009

The right of Julian Johnson to be identified as the
Author of this work has been asserted by him in accordance
with the Copyright, Designs and Patents Act 1988

ISBN 978–1–85168–687–2

Typeset by Jayvee, Trivandrum, India
Cover design by A. Meaden
Printed and bound in Great Britain by Bell & Bain, Glasgow

Oneworld Publications
185 Banbury Road
Oxford OX2 7AR
England
www.oneworld-publications.com

Learn more about Oneworld. Join our mailing list to
find out about our latest titles and special offers at:

www.oneworld-publications.com

Mixed Sources
Product group from well-managed
forests and other controlled sources
www.fsc.org   Cert no. TT-COC-002769
© 1996 Forest Stewardship Council

For my students – who taught me much.

Contents

Preface

What kind of book is this and who is it for? A 'Beginner's Guide' it may be, but it won't tell you where to begin. The fact that you've even picked up this book and started to read the Preface suggests that you're not a complete beginner at all, that you've already begun to listen to, be curious about, or are involved at some level in playing or singing classical music. In that sense, you and I are engaged in the same quest – not just to know more about this massively diverse body of music, spanning some thousand years or more, but to try to understand it better. To that end, what I've offered in this book are some frameworks within which classical music might be better understood.

This is not a history of music, though my chapters divide along broadly historical lines. It is not an introduction to key composers, musical works or techniques, though plenty of these appear along the way. There are literally scores of books that will give you an overview of all of this, with glossy pictures of musical instruments, composers and their contemporaries. Some come with CDs of music examples. All of these have their value and use, so why read this one?

This one is primarily concerned with what music has meant to people – why it mattered so much at the time, and why it might still matter to us now. Rather than tell a story in which musical style 'just changes' over the centuries, as if composers simply got bored with the old ways, I have tried instead to give a sense of how music has related to some of the big ideas of Western experience – spirituality, human emotion, the invention of the new, the weight of history, the self-identity of individuals and nations. Huge claims have been made for the meaning of classical music, framed in terms of religion, philosophy, psychology or politics. At other times, it's simply been taken as an innocent pleasure, a diversion or entertainment.

Talking about music is no substitute for listening to it. At the end of the book I have given a list of some key musical works that are either mentioned in the text or would illustrate the points I have tried to make. There are hundreds of other works that I might have suggested instead, so similar works by the same composers would do the job just as well if you find it difficult to get hold of the ones I've suggested. I have also recommended some books for further reading but these are best followed up in tandem with listening to the music. I have often found, with music that is new to me, that listening to it provokes questions, which sets me thinking and then reading, which sends me back to listen to the music again. It's a never-ending process which, at best, continually enriches the experience of the music.

But there is no right way. Some of my most vivid musical encounters have been by accident and some of the music that haunts me now is music that a few years ago did nothing for me. There is little to be gained by trying to listen chronologically – like the man who tried to read the whole of 'great' literature starting methodically with authors beginning with 'A', you won't get far. If I have any recommendation it is simply to follow your nose, stop at the places that interest you, but don't be afraid of the unfamiliar. Life often seems too short to listen to music that isn't immediately engaging; on the other hand, it's too short not to.

1

What is classical music?

If you browse through the 'classical' section of a major music outlet (on the high street or online) you're likely to find an eclectic collection of music – not just famous composers of the concert hall and opera house from the past few hundred years, but a host of lesser known figures and musical styles. For a start, you'll find an extensive range of music stretching way back through the Renaissance and medieval period to the simple unaccompanied religious chants of the ninth century or even earlier; next to Mozart, Tchaikovsky, Puccini and Debussy, you'll find music by Monteverdi, Palestrina, Machaut and Pérotin. At the other end of the historical spectrum, the 'classical music' section might include the music of film composers like John Barry or John Williams, songs drawn from pop and jazz idioms but performed by classical singers in orchestral arrangements, and a modernist avant-garde that sounds like it would be unlikely to appeal to the same people as Haydn or Schubert.

There is no simple definition of what constitutes classical music. The term refers to music drawn from over a thousand years of music history, from the medieval to the postmodern. It includes music written specifically for the concert hall but also music that was never intended for an audience. Though the best-known composers of the classical tradition were mostly working in Western Europe, today the story of classical music reaches across the globe. For many people, classical music is simply old music, yet many contemporary composers, writing in modern styles, see themselves as part of a continuing classical tradition. For some, classical music might be simply music for classically trained musicians – sung by choirs or played by the kind of acoustic instruments you find in orchestras. But the closer one looks the more elusive becomes any kind of definition. It's not just music written by dead composers because it's a living form; it doesn't have any particular set of rules or conventions because composers have continually altered these throughout history; it's not just music that takes itself seriously and calls itself 'art' because much of it was neither written nor performed in that way.

So how does over a thousand years of Western music come to be summed up by the term *classical*? What is there in common between the unaccompanied melodies sung by a few monks in empty chapels in the ninth century and a modern symphony written for an orchestra of a hundred musicians and performed to an audience of two thousand in the twenty-first century? A simple answer might be – not much. It quickly becomes clear that there are no firm definitions of classical music and it's rather futile to look for them. In one sense, classical music is simply the music that is taken to be classical music. This is a useful definition because it underlines that the category is a cultural and historical one and therefore changeable; it has to do with how music is framed, thought about and used, rather than with some essential and mysterious ingredient that classical pieces possess and others do not.

Nor is the idea of a classical music unique to western Europe. Similar musical repertoires were developed in the court cultures of China, Japan, Malaysia, Thailand and India. The institutions of professional musicians, musical notation and fixed musical repertories ensured a kind of continuity and uniformity of practice over centuries that these traditions have in common. Such a music does not usually happen in a society dominated by the basic material demands of food and shelter. More often than not, what we call art has been the product of lives granted a level of freedom from the basic demands of subsistence. Art and music have flourished in those periods of history, and those parts of society, in which the luxury of free time and material wealth has allowed such a culture to take precedence over more material matters. In the medieval world, it was thus primarily in the closed communities of the church and monastery and royal courts that music, literature and learning were able to flourish. It was not until the eighteenth century that this situation changed to any great extent, and the rise of an economically independent middle class meant that music making and concert going became a public activity for anyone who cared to buy a ticket or take music lessons.

It is worth remembering that the idea of classical music widely accepted today did not exist until about 300 years ago. Performing music in concert halls to a paying audience, as something inherently pleasurable and significant, was pretty much unheard of until the eighteenth century and not widely established until the nineteenth. The concert hall, the audience, and the idea of 'masterpieces' of classical music, were all effectively invented during the course of the eighteenth century – in London, Paris, Vienna, Berlin and other European cities. Much of the music that is now performed in public concerts was not composed for that purpose. The cantatas of J. S. Bach, for example, were written to be sung in religious services at the Church of St Thomas in Leipzig where Bach was cantor. These pieces were part of weekly worship, and included chorales (hymns) for the congregation to join in with the singing. Sing along during a modern concert hall performance of one of these works today and you're likely to be told to shut up.

Recording

Music that was originally written for the concert hall may today appear on the soundtrack to an advert or film. Conversely, music originally written for films is sometimes performed live in the concert hall. Rather than being bewildered by all this, it's probably best to accept that since the whole idea of a classical music is itself a historical invention, it's not surprising to find that it is still changing today. Nothing has changed music over the last century more radically than the invention and dissemination of recording technologies. Though Thomas Edison developed the phonograph in 1877, and wax cylinders were used as early as the 1880s for recording music, commercial recordings of music were not widely available until after the First World War. From the mid-1980s onwards, the vinyl disc gradually gave way to the new technology of the CD, yet just a decade later the MP3 file was already displacing the CD as the favoured way to handle recorded music. Today, children have more music stored on their phones, ipods or computers than would have been contained on all the yards of library shelves of a proud 'record collector' of the twentieth century.

The impact of recording technologies on how we think about and use music has been huge. Without doubt it has been the single most important historical shift in music since the development of the idea of the public concert in the eighteenth century. Before recording, music was a social event – it involved one or more people coming together to make music. Music lasted for as long as they sang or played and then it was over. Music happened only when and where there were people to make it. Before the modern concert took off, music tended to be restricted to compositions by recent or living musicians, probably working in the locality; it was rare to hear music from a distant time, place or culture. Even when music became professionalized, listening to music generally involved going to a specific venue, at a specific time, to hear musicians create a one-off event.

Recording changed all of that. Today's technology makes almost all the world's music instantly and constantly available to anyone with access to simple and cheap electronic gadgets for playing it. Music thus floats free of any specific occasion or venue, any particular time or place. It no longer has to be associated with a particular audience or group of musicians. For the first time, music (any music) can be an entirely personal affair. This is one of the reasons that the 'classical' label becomes harder to pin down. One of its distinctive aspects – a performance space defined by concert halls and opera houses – is dissolved by digital recording formats that means all music, classical music included, can become a personal soundtrack for commuting, exercising, shopping, or whatever you choose. The ubiquity of music as recorded sound means that it's very easy to overlook perhaps the most definitive aspect of the classical music tradition – the fact that it is a *written* or *notated* music. Though classical music may lack a precise definition today and mean quite different things to different people, at its heart is the idea of a music that has survived down the centuries because it was written down in some form. The origins of what music historians think of as classical music is more or less contemporary with the origins of a system of musical notation. Put very simply, the history of classical music in all its varied forms, is the history of a tradition that grew out of the possibilities of musical notation.

Notation

To a non-musician, notation might seem no more than an aid to memory, the only way of 'making a record' of how a piece goes, before the invention of electronic means of recording. This was certainly the original impetus behind the development of notational systems from about the ninth century onwards. Those responsible for singing religious services in cathedrals and monasteries in medieval Europe had to learn by heart a huge repertory of chants; indeed, it was estimated to take a singer some ten years to learn the entire repertory. So the first attempts to notate music were rather approximate memory aids, depicting the rough outline of melodic shapes, rather than specifying precise pitches and rhythms as modern notation does.

For some musicians today, notation remains a way of writing down music that has already been put together in performance. A good deal of pop music is either not notated at all, or done so only in sketched form – like a set of chords that players 'realize' in various ways in performance. While you can buy the sheet music for your favourite rock songs, or even transcriptions of your favourite jazz pianist, these are made after the event rather than being a set of instructions that the musicians play from, as is the case in classical practice. So much music today is made directly in the studio, not just recorded digitally via computer software, but with many of its sounds generated electronically, that the idea of notation simply evaporates as irrelevant.

The new technologies of the music studio mark a significant departure from the formative role played by notation in the classical tradition. One way of defining classical music, which has marked it out from other musical practices, is that it has been very largely a 'literary' musical culture, as opposed to an oral one. Like literature, classical music has been fixed in the act of writing in a way that distinguishes it from oral traditions of storytelling or folk music practices. The retelling of a story across different generations in an oral culture is as different to a nineteenth-century novel (fixed in every detail in its printing), as the reworking of a folksong or a jazz tune might be compared to a classical symphony. This idea of fixing a work in all its details (whether a novel or a symphony) is central to the idea of a classical canon, in the first place because it creates the idea of a 'work' that is the product of a specific, individual artist (the 'great writer' or 'great composer'). It then follows that the history of classical music, like the history of literature or painting, becomes the history of great works and the artists who made them.

But whether music is notated is not an arbitrary matter. Even early in its development in the Middle Ages, notation allowed for a more complex process of musical composition than playing or singing by ear alone. Notation allowed composers not only to rework and refine their musical ideas over time, it allowed them to develop longer and more complex forms, often made of several layers which could be laid down by the composer in a way that was unthinkable before notation. Works like *Spem in alium* (*c.*1570) by the Elizabethan composer Thomas Tallis, or *The Rite of Spring* (1913) by Stravinsky, depend upon the effect of multiple parts that only become available and manageable by means of notation. The idea of polyphony itself (of many voices working in harmony with each other), central to so much classical music, developed in tandem with ways of notating music more accurately. The notation was developed in order to accommodate the new polyphonic music of the thirteenth and fourteenth centuries, but, at the same time, the new music was shaped by what notation made possible.

It is hard to overestimate the importance of notation for what we think of today as classical music. Not only has it made possible the technical developments of rhythm, harmony, polyphony and extended musical forms for large ensembles of instrumentalists and singers, it has also shaped the idea of a work that is 'written' by a composer but 'performed' by someone else. It lies behind something that classical music simply takes for granted – that music is composed and performed – two quite separate activities. This is not the case in many other musical cultures where the musicians simply play their own music or sing their own songs. The idea of classical performance – the performance of pre-composed musical scores – presumes an audience and, from the eighteenth century onwards, it became the normative way of hearing classical music to assemble in a special venue to listen silently and passively to a musical performance.

The tradition of concert going associated with classical music is shaped overwhelmingly around the idea of 'great works' from the past, revisited time and again by new performers. The audience goes both to revisit the great work but also to hear what a particular performer will bring to bear upon it. Of course, new works and even old, rediscovered works are added, at the same time as some works or composers fall out of this canon of musical masterpieces. What has remained a constant for the idea of classical music, however, for a few hundred years now, is the idea of this pantheon of the greatest works and composers. The idea is underwritten not just by performances but also an extensive literature about music – books on the appreciation of music, history of music, biographies and critical interpretations of music, popular books as well as works of academic scholarship. Western classical music must be the most thought about, written about and theorized music in world history. This is possible because notation, for better or worse, has made it possible to think about 'the music' as something larger than any one performance of it. One can talk in general about Beethoven's 'Spring' Sonata or Verdi's *Otello*, without necessarily making reference to any one performance of it. Notation suggests that the work somehow 'exists' apart from its performance, despite the fact that, for most listeners, the work only exists while it is sounding – in performance.

Contemporary value

It is salutary to ask why we still listen to music that comes from such different times and places. Why do we fill our free time with music that comes from nineteenth-century Germany, or seventeenth-century Italy, or twelfth-century France? This is quite different to our interest in the relics of antiquity seen in a museum or visiting the ruins of an old monastery. We might be fascinated by the Elizabethan period of English history but we don't normally start dressing in the style of the period, adopting the language of the time, or reverting to Tudor standards of plumbing or personal hygiene. Why do we invest so heavily in a novel or a symphony written by and for people two centuries before we were born, when in the rest of life the most recent seems so desirable? And how is it that music from such very different lives and times can affect us just as powerfully, often more powerfully, than music of our own time?

The idea of classical music, like the idea of art more generally, assumes that the value of artworks exceeds their origins; listening to Beethoven's music is a different order of activity to simply looking at his letters in a museum or reading Viennese newspapers from the year 1800. We return to music written in quite different places, in quite different times and for quite different people, because they still seem to speak to us in ways that remain powerfully engaging. We might find them emotionally stirring or merely delightful, thought-provoking or just entertaining, but they draw us back in ways that seem to close up the years of history that separate our own world from the one in which they were made. Or perhaps the opposite is the case – and the source of their appeal – that we enjoy precisely the sense of distance from our own world that this music creates.

It is clear that we use this music in quite different ways to how it was intended. The fact that, for almost all of us, music is accessed overwhelmingly through some kind of recording technology means that music becomes part of our everyday life and environment. This is completely different to the experience of the medieval ecclesiastic hearing plainchant in the cathedral, the courtier participating in dancing in an Elizabethan masque, or the Neapolitan shopkeeper hearing a Rossini opera for the first time from the top of a hot and noisy opera house. The different context, the different experience of our own ears and eyes and minds, inevitably alters how we read musical works from the past. I can listen to a Mass setting from the fourteenth century while driving on the motorway at 70 mph, or sing along with my favourite Puccini arias in the shower. That changes the ways in which they become meaningful.

But why should you care about any of this? Perhaps you've picked up this book because you're simply intrigued by the music and want to know more about it. Arguments about music are rightly silenced by the music itself. Thought about music is productive and worthwhile only if you keep going back to the music. Though I have divided the chapters that follow this according to broad historical periods, classical music is not a history lesson, nor is it 'about' ideas – though it relates to both history and ideas. It is, first and foremost, an activity that engages us on a sensual, experiential level. Music does something to us and with us. It offers us ways of feeling and ways of ordering our experience of the world.

The vast repertoire of music we call classical music is perhaps just that – a repertoire of ways in which we might order our experience of the world. I listen to sixteenth-century polyphony and I have a sense of the timeless space of the divine; I listen to Beethoven and I sense the energy and urgency of self-becoming and striving towards goals; I listen to Ravel and I sense the irreducible particularity of living in this moment, this here and now; I listen to some contemporary electro-acoustic music and I have a sense of the sublime at the edge of the known world. Music speaks with many voices, and it says many things, but the sum of these voices constitutes a world richer than any of us will assimilate in a lifetime.

2
Sounding the divine: from the Middle Ages to 1600

Visiting one of the great medieval cathedrals of Europe – Notre Dame in Paris, Reims, Chartres, Canterbury, Lincoln – it is still possible today to feel the overwhelming effect such buildings must have had when they were built, some 800 years ago. Even for us, who take for granted the modern city and its technologies, entering the echoing space of a Gothic cathedral evokes a powerful sense of awe and wonder. No doubt this is partly to do with the scale of such a huge enclosed space and the way its vertical lines lead the gaze upwards to the implausibly high vaulted ceilings. It is partly to do with the use of light and distance, and partly to do with the abrupt change of environment as you leave the noisy bustle of the street behind and step inside the containment of the building. The cumulative effect of all these things, combined with the richness of the stained glass, the tapestries, the sculpture, evokes a powerful response even from the modern non-believer. In the first instance, just as it might have been in medieval times, the power of the building is felt as a massive aesthetic hit.

While the marvels of medieval architecture are what literally draw the eye, we are also profoundly affected (if less consciously) by its acoustic quality. The effect of reverberation and resonance produces a kind of aural equivalent to the sense of timelessness achieved by the building's physical space. This resonance, in which sound seems to expand rather than fade, is the starting point for the religious music of the medieval world. The sound of the human voice, familiar and mundane elsewhere, takes on a new tone here. The singing of religious texts, to simple unaccompanied melodic lines (know as plainsong or plainchant) must have seemed then, as it still does today, to transform mere words and speech into something far more mysterious. The spiritual quality associated with both the music and the architecture is rooted in the worldly, but seems to take off from it. The huge arches of the cathedral draw upwards but are rooted in the ground, just as lines of plainsong rise out of the ground of an intoning note. The arches of these melodic lines are shaped by the limits of the human voice and breath, and yet their cumulative effect, echoing long after the voice has ceased, seems to reach beyond the human.

The medieval period saw an astonishing exploration of this capacity of the human voice. While the religious texts of the Christian Church remained a fixed point of departure, the musical elaborations that sprung from them are evidence of a remarkable flowering of the human spirit. In endlessly creative ways, singers and composers of these centuries generated rich and complex musical responses that must have transported the medieval listener just as powerfully as the physical impact of the great cathedrals. Given that most medieval churchgoers were unable to read at all, let alone to read liturgical texts in Latin, the sensuous beauty of the sound of the singing voice in the echoing acoustic of these vast buildings must have been, as it remains now, intoxicating. Modern life is so over-rich in stimulants – in sound, colour, materials, food, speed – it is hard for us to appreciate quite how powerful an effect must have been created by the collection of sensual richness in these buildings. To modern ears, the unison singing of a single, unaccompanied melodic line, without harmony or obvious rhythm, might at first seem strangely bare, yet it still strikes us powerfully. It is, perhaps, precisely *because* of its relative simplicity, that it seems to speak, offering a kind of focused intensity so often absent in a modern culture where everything seems to be shouted.

Sacred monody

The term monody refers to any kind of music that consists of only a single musical line or part. It may be sung by one singer alone (as in a folksong, say, or a lullaby), or it may be sung by many voices in unison (as in the singing of a national anthem in a sports stadium). A piece for solo flute, such as Debussy's *Syrinx*, is a monody, just as much as a rendition of 'Danny Boy' by a solitary singer. A musical piece is a monody so long as there are no other parts that depart from the principal line to add harmonic or rhythmic contrast. There are surprisingly few universals in world music, but the importance of a single unaccompanied voice is one of them. The impulse to raise the voice in song, alone or collectively, remains a fundamental one across the world's diverse musical styles and traditions. That said, music in the modern world is most often characterized precisely by the combination of different instruments and voices in different parts. The ways in which musicians have done that in the West date back approximately a thousand years, and it is to that time that music historians return to think about the origins of a music which we later came to think of as 'classical'.

Before the tenth century we can safely assume that all music was effectively monodic. Singers may have been joined by all kinds of instruments but merely as a way of rounding out the sound of a single line melody. Because of the absence of reliable evidence our picture of music before this time is necessarily rather conjectural. There seems to have been a ready exchange of musical style between the religious chant melodies and songs sung outside the church – an easy-going relationship that continued, off and on, through most of the Middle Ages. The chants of the early Christian Church almost certainly derived from earlier Jewish chants, as well as regional folk traditions. Given the huge geographical area covered by the Church, even in the first few centuries AD, there were necessarily some significant regional variations in religious music. Scholars have identified quite distinct chant styles, for example, in the outposts of the early Church stretched out around the Mediterranean from Greece and Turkey to Egypt and North Africa.

Towards the end of the eighth century there was a concerted effort to impose some uniformity on the diverse musical practices of the early Church, as part of a larger attempt to impose a central authority across the Holy Roman Empire. The Emperor Charlemagne (742–814) banned the regional Gallican chant of France, insisting it should be replaced by the Roman practice (in Spain, so-called Mozarabic chant managed to continue until the eleventh century before it too was officially proscribed). The centralization of religious authority was of course also one of political authority; an agreed ritual practice, in terms of text and music, was imposed from Rome on all religious institutions within the ambit of the Holy Roman Empire. The chants to which liturgical texts were sung in church services were now taught by instructors trained in Rome. The new uniformity of chant that resulted came to be known as 'Gregorian chant', even though Pope Gregory I (pope from 590) had died nearly two centuries before it was achieved. In many ways this was a marketing ploy of the Church reformers, passing off an authoritarian and political move of the contemporary Church as the work of a highly popular and esteemed figure from history. It is one that stuck, nevertheless, as you will find if you look for a recording of early plainchant today.

So what exactly is plainchant? Aside from being a single line, sung melody, the first aspect of it that strikes the modern listener is that it is an 'unmeasured' music, without any obvious beat or rhythm. Its flexible, flowing style derives directly from the text that is being sung. In the simplest chants, where every syllable of the text has a melodic note, this is relatively straightforward. Some chants have two or three notes per syllable however, and in the so-called 'florid' style a single syllable of text might be sung to a long string of notes (called a *melisma*). Clearly, in the syllabic kind the text takes priority; the music heightens the tone of the voice, but does not obscure the words that are being sung. In the florid or melismatic style, however, the music begins to take priority over the words. Listening to a single word – like 'Alleluia' – delivered through a long string of notes to each syllable, one is very likely to lose track of the word altogether.

In general, as one might expect, the Church authorities insisted that the words should be clearly audible, but this demand tended to be made only periodically and in the face of a musical practice that clearly delighted in elaboration for its own sake. The tension between the two – the clarity of the words and the rich elaboration of the music – defines the history of Church music. It is interesting to note that early Church leaders specifically allowed the music to 'take off' from the words at certain points in the liturgy. Pope Damasus, for example, whose pontificate lasted from 366 to 384, described the 'jubilus' (the florid end of the Alleluia section of the Mass) in terms that seemed to give music free rein. 'By the term jubilus', he wrote, 'we understand that which neither in words nor syllables nor letters nor speech is it possible to express or comprehend how much man ought to praise God'. St Augustine, in one of the earliest medieval treatises on music, *De Musica* (389), described it in even more extreme terms: 'It is a certain sound of joy without words ... the expression of a mind poured forth in joy ... A man rejoicing in his own exultation, after certain words which cannot be understood, bursts forth into sounds of exaltation without words, so that it seems that he, filled with excessive joy, cannot express in words the subject of that joy.'

Listening to medieval plainsong today, with our ears conditioned by the rhythmic regularity of baroque and classical music, it is hard not to be struck by the fluidity of the melodic line and the natural freedom that this gives to the voice compared with the rational order and uniformity of later instrumental music. It is a wonderful paradox that although the simplicity of the unaccompanied voice implies a monastic kind of asceticism, the effect it produces is powerfully sensuous. Though the comparison has often been made, its effect is something like that of a medieval illuminated manuscript, in which a simple written text lifts off the page by means of the richness of its colours and calligraphic design. It is hardly surprising, therefore, that the singing of plainchant was closely related to the religious mysticism that lay at the heart of the medieval monastic movement. One of the most extraordinary 'discoveries' of recent years has been the music of Hildegard of Bingen (1098–1179) – a rare example of a named composer from the twelfth century, even rarer in that Hildegard was a woman. The Abbess of a Benedictine convent in the Rhine valley, Hildegard was not only one of the great musicians of her age, but a writer of important works on theology, natural history and medicine. About eighty of her compositions have survived, including a morality play for women's voices, *Ordo Virtutum*. Like other mystics of her age, she recorded a series of intense religious visions, the rapturous quality of which informs her plainchants. Often demanding an extended vocal range from the singer, the ascending contour of these melodies seems, to many listeners, to capture a sense of spiritual ecstasy that still communicates powerfully a thousand years after they were written.

This association between medieval chant and mysticism is deep-seated and not to be confused with the modern marketing of CDs that blurs the difference between spirituality and relaxation. There are good reasons for the link that go well beyond the immediate impression of 'timelessness' conveyed by the ancient origins of this music. It has to do with the nature of the music itself. Firstly, the absence of the kind of mechanical regularity of beat that dominates so much music in the modern world confers a kind of organic freedom and suppleness to the musical line. Secondly, rather than being shaped by the *tonal* goals of a more modern harmonic system, plainchant elaborates a *modal* scale that creates a less directed, more contained sense of time. The shape of each individual phrase, and of the whole piece, is less concerned with the later romantic obsession with building up to successive emotional climaxes and far more concerned with elaboration – more like the overlapping petals of a flower than the storyline of a narrative piece. Thirdly, plainchant foregrounds a certain quality of the singing voice like no other music in the Western tradition. The nature of the melodic phrases, the texts which they set, and the resonant acoustic of stone buildings in which they were sung, produce a distinctive style of singing in which purity of tone is everything. There is nothing to distract from the centrality of the singing voice here – no accompaniment and no contrast of instruments or voices.

Of course, plainchant was directly linked with religious ideas and sentiments because it originated in the singing of religious services. It was in the great monastic institutions of the medieval world that these were most elaborated and strictly observed, with daily 'offices' or 'hours' marking out the day from lauds at daybreak to compline in the evening and matins in the middle of the night. The first monastic order in the West was founded by St Benedict (*c*.480–*c*.547), followed by the Dominican and Franciscan orders. Famous as centres of learning across Europe and beyond, the monasteries inevitably were also key centres for the development of music. It is primarily from monastic libraries that we have surviving manuscript sources for medieval music; the monks not only had the wealth and education necessary for the copying of musical manuscripts, they also had the richest musical traditions.

This can be seen in the way that new practices developed within the relatively closed societies of monasteries. While chants for the church offices were strictly codified, the creativity of successive generations continually elaborated upon them. Though it was prohibited to alter the chants themselves, a degree of freedom was found by adding florid additional passages at the beginning and ends of some of the liturgical chants, or sometimes as interpolations between the main parts of liturgical texts (called *tropes*). Because these florid, wordless melismas were hard to memorise, singers often ascribed texts to them, with a syllable to each note of the melisma. Though this began as a purely mnemonic device, as soon as the texts themselves were sung they became textual interpolations just as the trope had formed a purely musical one. Some of these passages were known as *sequences*. Examples have been found as early as the later ninth century at the monasteries of St Martial (Limoges) and St Gall (Switzerland). They became very popular, developing into hymns by the twelfth century in the work of musicians like Adam of St Victor. In fact, the threat posed by sequences to an orthodox and uniform liturgy was such that they were eventually outlawed by the Council of Trent in the sixteenth century.

Polyphony: Notre Dame

Perhaps the most striking change in medieval music was the appearance of a music in which the single voice (*monody*) was elaborated into several different voices (*polyphony*). There are many possible explanations as to how and why this happened, all of which may be partially true. The natural division of male and female voices, or unbroken boys' voices and men's voices, means that singing an octave apart would have been normal for a mixed group of singers even when singing the same melodic line. Group singing, especially in the context of a congregation rather than a trained choir, is apt to produce little differences in the same melody, as some voices move to the next note slightly sooner or later than others. The result can be a form of *heterophony* – the simultaneous delivery of slightly different versions of what is essentially the same melody. The free improvisation of a second melodic part over the chant may well have been another way in which the idea developed; the chants were such well-known melodies that it is highly probable that one singer might elaborate upon it while the remainder delivered the standard version. This is a recurrent instinct of performers throughout history and in many different traditions across the world.

It may not have been unusual to sing a plainchant over a *drone* – a fixed pitch or keynote either sung or sustained in an instrument. This has the effect of emphasizing the way in which the melodic line moves away from and then returns to a keynote, creating a powerful sense of arching away from and returning back to a starting point. The effect of the sustained note is to exert something like a gravitational pull upon the upper part which draws away from this 'ground', appears to take flight for a while, and then returns to rest. Though the harmonic system we know as modern tonality was not to be established until around 1600, it is nevertheless built upon this same sense of journeying and return, a temporal process shaped by the pleasure in the distance from the keynote traced out by each note of the melody.

Deliberate experimentation with adding another part to the chant probably began as early as *c.*900; surviving manuscripts from the monastery of St Gall in Switzerland show evidence of this, and it is mentioned in the medieval musical treatise, the *Musica enchiriadis (Musical Handbook)* of *c.*900, which suggests the practice was reasonably well established by then. Early forms of polyphony (*organum*) took various forms. In the simplest type, the melody was followed by another voice at a fixed pitch – usually a fourth higher. Imagine singing a well-known tune (starting on C, say) and asking someone else to sing exactly the same tune at the same time but starting on F – you are now performing basic organum. As is clear from how the process arises, it is essentially about expanding a line of music through elaboration in another line. It has nothing to do with modern ideas of harmony, which are about how notes sound together at any one moment (understood 'vertically' in a musical score).

This note-against-note type of organum was called *discant organum*. The idea persists today in the idea of a 'descant' melody, typically added to the final verse of a Christmas carol by the sopranos of the choir. Because the basic interval between the two parts was a fourth or fifth, medieval organum can sound dry or even discordant to our ears, since our modern sense of harmony is shaped around the third, an interval that medieval theorists considered to be dissonant. In passing, we might note how this discrepancy underlines that the question of what is consonant and what is dissonant in music has less to do with acoustics and physics and far more to do with cultural and historical definitions of music. In *florid organum* the chant was given in long notes while an upper voice sang shorter notes against each melody note, a practice that dates from *c.*1100. The voice that held the slow-moving plainchant melody was called the 'tenor' (*tenere* – to hold) or *vox principalis* (principal voice) against which the florid 'organalis' part weaved another line. The practice became widespread: the *Winchester Troper*, dating from the eleventh century, contains more than 150 examples of two-part organa, and sources from the monastery of St Martial in Limoges, from the first half of the twelfth century, show extended examples of the florid type.

The consolidation of early polyphony, however, is most famously associated with musicians working at the new cathedral of Notre Dame in Paris in the twelfth century. The building of the cathedral itself was begun in 1161 and not completed for nearly a hundred years, but it is clear that music flourished there in extraordinary ways from the start. Surviving from the late twelfth century is the *Magnus Liber Organi* – the great book of organum. The work of one of the first named composers of whom we have some record, Léonin, whose key work was accomplished *c*.1150–80, this book is based upon plainchants for every moment in the church calendar. A later edition, by his successor Pérotin, includes his own polyphonic versions of the chants, probably composed for feast days in 1198 and 1199. According to an Englishman (known ever since as 'Anonymous 4') who heard Pérotin's music at Notre Dame, even a third and fourth part was sometimes added to the chant melody.

Such coordination of different parts could not be accomplished without a rhythmic precision beyond that required by monodic plainchant. The twelfth century thus sees the beginning of a long process of developing ways to ensure that singers performing different lines would stay aligned with each other. Just as the idea of pitch was ordered by distinct modes, or scales, derived from ancient Greek modes, so too was rhythm ordered by schemes derived from classical Greek poetry – patterns of short and long, stressed and unstressed syllables. The larger phrase structure, as in all vocal music, is of course dictated by the limits imposed by what can be sung in a single breath, and these were increasingly marked in musical manuscripts, with a vertical line (the forerunner of the modern musical 'rest') dividing each separate phrase or section (known as *ordines*). Every gain in musical history is accompanied by a corresponding loss – the price paid for the development of one aspect of music is the decline of another. In this case, the coordination of two or more separate parts was achieved by breaking up the constant flow of monodic chant.

That said, it is almost impossible to overestimate the significance of the idea of polyphony for European culture. It was an idea of such magnitude that it effectively divides the second millennium AD from the first. It represents a flight of the musical imagination combined with an intellectual quality of invention that shaped the subsequent history of music. Listen to some examples of simple organa by Léonin and Pérotin, then fast forward through the fourteenth and fifteenth centuries, through the music of Machaut and Dufay, until you arrive at the great polyphonic masses of the sixteenth century (Palestrina, Victoria, Lassus, Tallis, Byrd) and you will get the picture. Something absolutely simple and focused – the monodic chant – is elaborated into something of almost ungraspable richness. At various points in the history of Western music the primacy of melody has reasserted itself but one of the most distinctive achievements of this tradition has always been the polyphonic combination of plural parts – different instruments and voices moving independently of each other yet all the while combining to form some harmonious whole, a multi-levelled richness which is more than the sum of its individual parts.

As St Augustine noted in the fourth century, music begins when the normal speaking voice is inadequate for what needs to be expressed, and the voice breaks out into the heightened tone of singing, when words alone give way to musical sound which has a life of its own, independent of any text it carries. The early monodies – both sacred and secular – embodied this idea. But the move to polyphony represents an exponential leap: it expands the singularity of the text, and the single voice that carries it, to a plural voice. Unlike the single voice of ordinary speech, music produced a blossoming outwards into a harmony constituted by several parts. Like the great rose window of

Notre Dame cathedral, music embodied the richness of a plural, roseate form, made up of multiple petals whose combined effect of line and colour overwhelmed and transported the onlooker. It constitutes a decisive moment in Western consciousness, when the constriction of words to a single line of thought at any one time, was broken open by the multiple voices of polyphonic music.

Secular music: songs of courtly love

But music was not confined to the Church. We can safely assume that there was plenty of music in the everyday, secular life of the Middle Ages. It does not survive in the historical record to the same extent as sacred music because it was rare for a secular musician to have either the need or the resources for the expensive process of transcribing a musical manuscript. Nevertheless, from those sources that have survived, a lively picture emerges, of music in the court and the marketplace, the town and the countryside, in public and private settings. The principal forms of early vocal music differed relatively little between sacred and secular contexts. What differed was, above all, the performance context and the language of the singing; whereas religious music was always in Latin, secular song was generally in the vernacular. The ease with which music crossed the divide between sacred and secular is well illustrated by the common practice of *contrafacta*, songs in which the original sacred texts had simply been replaced by secular ones – or vice versa. This might seem odd to us now because our 'modern' understanding of songs is that the music in some way expresses the words it sets, but the medieval attitude to the relationship of words and music was quite different.

What mattered more in defining different kinds of music was who was singing, and to whom. One can distinguish between different kinds of singers by the social status they occupied. The least stable and most socially marginal were the *jongleurs* – essentially poor, travelling musician-entertainers for whom performing tricks was as important as singing. Their wayfaring lifestyle almost certainly made them valuable as carriers of news from one region to another. A more educated group of itinerant musicians were the *goliards* – students and young men in minor holy orders who adopted the lifestyle of the wandering musician until they found a more permanent place in society. Their songs were often bawdy, sometimes moral, often immoral, and generally satirical at the Church's expense. After about 1225 their presence was much diminished with the founding of the first medieval universities. A flavour of the type of ribald poetry that formed the basis of their songs can be gleaned from looking at the text of Carl Orff's popular choral work *Carmina Burana*. Though this was composed in 1936, its texts were taken from a thirteenth-century manuscript discovered in a Bavarian monastery.

The most extraordinary flowering of secular song, however, was that of the *troubadours* (in south-western France) and the *trouvères* (in northern France). Whereas jongleurs were uneducated wayfarers on the fringes of society, troubadours and trouvères were courtly singers, either with a noble patron or, in many cases, noblemen themselves. Where the songs of the goliards were earthy and bodily, those of the troubadours and trouvères were noble and ideal. And the ideal that they sang about, over and again, was that of courtly love, or *fin' amors*. On one level, the fact that love songs dominated the secular musical culture of the Middle Ages might offer a link between our own tastes and those of some 800 years ago; unrequited desire, it seems, is pretty much timeless. But the courtly love tradition of medieval society was highly stylized and was shaped around the idea of the impossible distance and unavailability of the lover. A highly refined code of etiquette lay behind this cultivation of erotic longing such that even here, in what one might expect to be the furthest from religious music, there is a link with sacred hymns. The mystical hymns to the Virgin Mary or those drawing on the erotic language of the Song of Songs were essentially no different to the secular songs of the courtly love tradition; both were shaped around an impossible but infinite longing for the beloved.

The aristocratic musical culture of the troubadours flourished between about 1000 and 1200. They suffered considerably in the twenty-year massacre of the Albigensian Crusade (1209–29) designed to exterminate heretics in southern France. One of the many named individuals, and one of the most famous of all troubadours, was Bernart de Ventadorn. His patron was Eleanor of Aquitaine, whom he followed to northern France for her first marriage and accompanied to England in 1152 for her second, to Henry of Anjou, who subsequently became Henry II of England. Some forty-five of his poems have survived, eighteen of them with music intact. We know of such individuals and their music because, although the troubadour tradition was an oral one, their songs were written down retrospectively and collected in *chansonniers*, anthologies of troubadour songs produced from the mid-thirteenth century. These also included biographies (*vidas*) of the singers themselves, from which it was clear that this aristocratic genre was not confined to male singers but included many female poet-singers too (known as *trobairitz*).

In northern France the trouvères flourished between about 1100 and 1300. One of the most famous was Adam de la Halle, whose works include not only lyric songs but narrative forms too. His play with music 'Le jeu de Robin et de Marion' (1283) is sometimes cited as the earliest opera (though strictly that term is not really used until about 1600). In Germany, the courtly love tradition was carried by the so-called Minnesänger. One of their number, Walter von der Vogelweide (d.*c.*1230), turns up over 600 years later as a character in Richard Wagner's opera

Die Meistersinger von Nürnberg, another as the hero of his opera *Tannhäuser*, which also includes the figure of Wolfram von Eschenbach, author of the medieval epic poem 'Parzifal'. Wagner here conflated two quite separate historical traditions of secular song – the noble courtly love songs of the twelfth and thirteenth centuries and the later, middle-class song tradition of the guilds as represented by Hans Sachs in the sixteenth century.

Across Europe, sacred and secular song fed off each other. Examples are found in Italy where the dominant form was the *lauda*, a type of religious song to a non-liturgical text. In Spain, similar songs were called *cantigas* and often featured texts about miracles associated with the Virgin Mary. The *laude spirituali* was essentially a group marching song, something sung by pilgrims perhaps, but was also key to the highly influential penitential movement of the fourteenth century. The German equivalent was the so-called *Geisserlied* or flagellation song. Its widespread use as part of a vicious code of self-flagellation became of such concern to the Church that it was eventually outlawed. Though the musical techniques between sacred and secular song may not have differed significantly, an important aspect of this flowering of secular forms was the development of vernacular poetry with which it developed in tandem. The troubadours wrote highly stylized poetry in the Provencal or Occitan language (hence 'langue d'Oc' and the region of modern southern France known as Languedoc).

The rise of the composer

The modern idea of the composer, shaped by images of romantic genius from Beethoven onwards, has little to do with the musical life of medieval times. It was in the nature of church music, and the codification of liturgical music in particular, to preclude the idea of value being attached to the creativity of the individual. Just as the sacred texts of the liturgy were not to be altered, so their musical settings were hardly to be altered by individuals. The touchstone of our modern view of the composer is almost always the idea of expression – expression of the individual, embodied by the composer himself – but this too is largely alien to the medieval worldview. Nevertheless, as we have seen, certain individuals did accrue considerable fame in their own lifetimes or posthumously – such as Bernart de Ventadorn or Adam de la Halle.

It was not until the fourteenth century, however, that we meet a composer whose influence on the development of musical technique and subsequent influence on other composers marks him out as one of the first 'great' composers in the modern mould. The period from around 1300 is generally known as the *Ars nova* – a self-conscious designation of 'newness' underlined in a treatise of that name written in 1322 by Philippe de Vitry. Distinguishing itself from the *Ars antica*, the new age was characterized by a flowering of secular culture in the face of increasing criticism of a corrupt Church (the latter was famously lampooned in the highly influential anti-clerical fable of the *Roman de Fauvel*). The esteem of the Church reached something of a low point in the time of the Great Schism (1378–1417) when two separate Popes, one in Rome and one in Avignon, both sustained their separate claims to be the one true elected representative of God on earth. At the same time, Europe was ravaged by The Hundred Years War (1339–1453) and the Black Death; the latter killed over twenty-five million people, including half the population of Great Britain. The impotence of the Church, mired in internal politics and corruption, forms part of the background to the huge growth in secular culture and art of this period. One of the most important forms of this was the flowering of vernacular literature in the work of writers such as Chaucer, Dante, Petrarch and Boccaccio.

In music the new attitude was exemplified in the astonishing figure of Guillaume de Machaut (*c.*1300–77), perhaps the first figure that we might treat in a similar way to the idea of a 'great composer' of the later classical tradition. It seems that Machaut himself was not unaware of his own importance, since towards the end of his life he arranged for his entire work to be copied out in a particularly extravagant style – an extraordinary thing to do in the fourteenth century. In part, this reflects his relatively high social status – he was Secretary to John of Luxembourg, King of Bavaria, a canon of Reims Cathedral, and a leading poet in his own right (whose work was admired by Chaucer). Though a priest, Machaut wrote almost entirely secular music. Of some 140 extant pieces, only a handful are liturgical (six motets and *La Messe de Notre Dame*, the latter written in the 1360s and probably the earliest setting of the Mass as a whole).

A central part of his secular music was the continuation of the courtly love tradition in poetry and song setting. Some of Machaut's songs set parts of his own immense love poem *Le Livre dou Voir Dit*, whose more than nine thousand lines document the relationship between the author (then over sixty years old) and his adolescent admirer, Peronne. The style is well demonstrated by the opening verses of one his many courtly love songs, 'Dame, de qui toute ma joie vient'.

'DAME, DE QUI TOUTE MA JOIE VIENT' (GUILLAUME DE MACHAUT)

Lady, from whom comes all my joy,
I cannot love or cherish you too much.
Nor praise, serve, fear, honour or obey
You as much as is fitting.

For the kind hope,
Sweet lady, which I have of seeing you,
Gives me a hundred times more joy and happiness
Than I could deserve in a hundred thousand years.

Modern listeners will be disappointed, however, if they expect to find the same sort of emotional response that a romantic composer might make to such a text. In both secular and sacred vocal music, the words often provided no more than phonetic material for what was essentially a more abstract musical elaboration. Listen, for example, to the opening Kyrie of Machaut's *Le Messe de Nostre Dame*. The words are virtually absent, because the single opening syllable is stretched out apparently infinitely by the voices, only occasionally punctuated by points of rest. What modern ears might dismiss as rather shapeless, meandering lines, without obvious phrase structure, can also be heard as a quiet but ecstatic process of unfolding, in which overlapping parts expand a sense of vast space. To the medieval mind, this would have been an astonishing aural counterpart to the physical space of Reims cathedral in which the piece was performed.

In many ways, the music leaves its words behind. The opening recitation of a phrase of plainchant at the start of the Credo, for example, is merely the starting point for a purely musical and polyphonic elaboration. The rational order of the word is wonderfully superseded by a medieval spirituality that finds its voice in this music – a flowering that a later, more rational age was to suppress.

Machaut was the first of the great 'northern' composers who dominated European music for some three centuries. While the visual arts flowered spectacularly in the city states of Italy in the fourteenth and fifteenth centuries (above all in Florence and Venice), the greatest centre of musical culture was the kingdom ruled by successive Dukes of Burgundy, a realm which included areas of what is now northern France, Luxembourg, Belgium and Holland, and which had its capital in Dijon. One of the most brilliant courts in Western Europe, its rich musical life was centred on a chapel choir modelled on that of the Papal Chapel in Rome. Composers at this time were invariably singers because singing was absolutely primary to musical culture until the much later rise in instrumental music in the seventeenth and eighteenth centuries. Until then, instrumentalists were generally associated with minstrels (i.e. a lower class of musician). Almost all of the key musical figures of this age were associated with the court of Burgundy: Dufay, Binchois, Ockeghem, Busnois, Josquin and Isaac.

The singular prominence of Machaut in the fourteenth century was followed exactly a century later by the figure of Guillaume Dufay (*c.*1400–74). Though by no means alone, Dufay's style exemplifies the musical achievements of his age; his music occupies a central place in the dominant musical style of what we now know as the Franco-Netherlandish school. He worked at Cambrai Cathedral but also travelled to Italy, where he was employed as a private musician by wealthy families, as well as by court chapels and by the Papal Chapel in Rome. The public importance of his music is underlined by the fact that many of his works were written to commemorate great events such as the signing of peace treaties, the dedication of churches and the election of popes, as well as more personal family events.

Dufay composed in the same three forms that dominated music for nearly three centuries, from Machaut to the late sixteenth century: the mass, the motet and the chanson. He wrote over seventy chansons, mostly for three voices. These are already more 'modern' in sound in that the upper part tends to be more important than the lower two, which contribute a sense of continuous motion and fill in the harmony underneath. There is a new sense of rhythmic freedom in Dufay's music too (with a free mixing up of duple and triple time) and a new sense of tonality that comes from a clearer sense of dividing the music by cadences.

The refinement of both the poetry and the music is telling about the nature of the society at the Burgundian court; the beautifully stylized language and cultivated artificiality provides perfect evidence that there was nothing rudimentary about medieval culture. Courtly love remains the single most important theme of these songs though Dufay, like his contemporaries, varied the tone of his music according to which kind of song he was writing – a ballade (for longer and more serious poems), or a virelai or rondeau (for less serious, dance songs). These three principal forms of song were differentiated by different patterns of repetition but were all based on the idea of verse and refrain as we would recognize it today.

The term motet derives simply from the French word 'mot', meaning 'word'. It reflects the importance of the tenor part formed from a pre-existing melody but set to new words. But it was a feature of the motet that more than one text was set at the same time, sometimes two texts in two different languages, or one secular and one sacred. Such polytexuality underlines again that the attitude to word setting in early music was quite different to what we meet in later music – such as the nineteenth century Lied for example, or the Italian madrigal around 1600, where a close fit between poetic meaning and musical expression is the basis of the genre. It also reminds us that such music was not really intended for an audience or a congregation; this was music written for its own sake, for the delight of those who sang it and for the glory of God to whom it was directed.

Some of Dufay's motets were written for grand state occasions, like 'Supremum est mortalibus bonum' (written in the 1430s). One of the most complex and impressive is 'Nuper rosarum flores', written for the dedication of Florence Cathedral in 1436. These works are good examples of the medieval fascination with abstract numerical schemes realized in musical form. One of the most important techniques embodying this idea was that of *isorhythm* (literally, 'the same rhythm'), which finds a late flowering in the work of Dufay. It is based on the idea of a rhythmic pattern (called a *talea*) repeated one or more times as the basis of the piece. It may be repeated exactly or in diminution (in shorter note values but preserving the same proportions) or augmentation (longer note values but preserving the same proportions). Sometimes it is just the tenor part that exhibits this feature, but it may involve all the voices. Because the *talea* may be very long (up to forty bars in some cases) this device is not necessarily recognizable by the listener, though the broader effect of the piece appearing to speed up (through diminution) or slowing down (through augmentation) is likely to be obvious.

While the rhythm of a voice part is organized by the *talea*, the pitches making up each line are also organized by a repeating pattern (called a *color*). The neat trick is that the lengths of the *talea* and *color* are different so they don't coincide. The result is something like a simple kaleidoscope, where the same colours and shapes return but in different combinations. It is interesting to note that some twentieth composers, such as Olivier Messiaen or Harrison Birtwistle, took up this idea (some 600 years after its heyday) as a structuring device in their own music.

Perhaps the most important device of medieval music, found in motets and Masses, was the *cantus firmus* – the pre-existing melody (usually a plainchant melody) sung in long notes (i.e. slowly) by the tenor, against which the composer wrote a counterpoint of other parts moving more rapidly. It underlines how different was the medieval conception of composition to a more modern one. The medieval composer laid down the different lines of a piece one after the other, starting with the *cantus firmus* for the whole piece. To this could be added a second line, making a satisfactory counterpoint with it at every juncture. Then a third, or even a fourth part could be added in the same way. Notice how the piece is conceived entirely horizontally, without worrying so much about the 'vertical' effect of harmony from moment to moment. Modern studio technology allows for a similar way of working, with each track being laid down separately for the whole song, like successive

Our modern conception of harmony was set out in Rameau's *Treatise of Harmony* of 1722. It codified a theory of chords formed over a bass line that is still current today. Go to the piano and play any chord. To us, it seems like an object, a thing – we call it a chord of C major, say. But this idea is a relatively modern invention. To a composer of the sixteenth century a chord simply didn't exist as a separate, individual object. Harmony arose from the movement of melodic lines, thought of 'horizontally' across the stave, not 'vertically' as chords began to be envisaged in the early eighteenth century. This shift from lines to chords, horizontal to vertical, was a massive change in musical thinking. It suggests a quite different way of experiencing not just music, but time.

layers of colour in screen printing. By contrast, composers from about 1600 onwards were much more likely to think about all the parts simultaneously; rather then write the viola part for a whole symphony before thinking about the violin part, Mozart would have considered the interaction of all the orchestral parts together, conceived 'vertically', as he wrote his symphony section by section.

The cantus firmus offered a powerful way of structuring a larger piece of music. In the composition of Masses it came to provide a way of binding together the separate movements into a larger unity. The so-called Cyclic Mass of the fifteenth and sixteenth centuries was thus achieved by basing each of the five main movements (Kyrie, Gloria, Credo, Sanctus, Agnus Dei) on the same cantus firmus. This was a major achievement of medieval music, signalling a concern with long-range structural thinking that pre-empts the large-scale works of the classical era. Surprisingly, the cantus firmus did not even have to be derived from a religious chant. Dufay was the first in a long line of composers who borrowed secular melodies as the structural foundation of their Masses. One of Dufay's most famous works, the *Missa L'homme armé* (written in the 1460s) takes its name from a famous and enduring popular song ('The armed man') which found its way into many subsequent musical works by many different composers. A decade or so earlier, in the 1450s, Dufay used one of his own chanson melodies as the basis of a Mass – the *Missa se la face ay pale*. Through Dufay, the cantus firmus principle became a foundation of the musical technique of the Franco-Netherlandish school, but he himself took it from the great English composer John Dunstable. It was not the only way in which continental music was influenced by English music at this time. In particular, the much admired sweetness of the English sound (a result of the English fondness for thirds in their music) was taken up by composers like Dufay and Binchois. The rich blend of voices achievable by a four-part texture now became standard, with a lower voice added under-neath the tenor (called a contra-tenor, but in effect the modern bass). The theorist Johannes Tinctoris claimed, in 1475, that music had been transformed into a totally 'new art' which rendered obsolete everything written earlier, and he singled out the English school and above all Dunstable as the basis of this achievement.

That new art was embodied in the work of Josquin des Prez (*c*.1450–1521), widely seen as a watershed in music history. He was a celebrity even in his own time and his works continued to be published and performed long after his death (something we take for granted about the idea of classical music but which was not at all common before around 1800). He composed about 100 motets, some 20 Masses and about 75 secular pieces. His achievement was to bring together the polyphonic style of the Burgundian composers and the harmonic sensibility of the Italians, resulting in a music with a greater sense of harmonic richness and direction. A new sensitivity to the vertical construc-tion of chords was part of a changing relationship between words and music that came to be one of the most important developments of the later sixteenth century.

This is evident in the way that Josquin's music works in smaller units; rather than a continuous outpouring of unbroken lines, his music is formed from chains of interlocking phrases. The music seems to breathe more, forming clear moments of pausing and rebeginning, with one part imitated by the next through all four voices. This produces a greater variety and contrast in the musical character and texture, a kind of freedom from the structural demands of the cantus firmus. The older way of composing 'successively', one line at a time, began to give way in Josquin to the more modern idea of 'simultaneous' composition in which all the parts were considered together. The result was a new equivalence of all four voice parts and the freedom to vary and break up the musical texture. Listen, for example, to a motet like 'Ave Maria'; each new line of text receives a different musical treatment, suggesting a carefully considered response to the words.

To be sure, the cantus firmus was still used, especially in the basses where the larger scale of the work demanded a more constructivist approach. But the emphasis here, as so often in music history, was less on the material itself than on what the composer did with it. Composers have always delighted in taking very ordinary material as the starting point of an extraordinary composition. (Beethoven's *Diabelli Variations* are a good example.) Two of Josquin's Masses are based on musical puns, as if to underline that the basic material was relatively arbitrary. The *Missa La sol fa re mi* (1502) advertises that it is based on no more than a string of five notes. The *Missa Hercules Dux Ferrariae* (c.1500) is based on a cantus firmus drawn from the musical letter names that can be extracted from the name of its aristocratic dedicatee, Ercole, Duke of Ferrara.

The dominance of the Franco-Netherlandish composers was not achieved by a few composers alone but by a host of other celebrated musicians, some of whom stayed in Flanders but many of whom also went to work in Italy. The chansons of

Gilles Binchois and Antonie Busnois or the masses of Johannes Ockeghem were produced without venturing abroad, whereas composers like Adrian Willaert, who became *maestro di capella* at St Mark's in Venice, was to have a huge influence on the next generation of Italian composers. Only English music retained a sense of independence from the influence of the Northerners, with a style that favoured florid and highly decorative counterpoint. The complex interplay of different voices, producing a sumptuous surface to the music, remained a distinct feature of English music through the fifteenth and sixteenth centuries, one partially recaptured in the revisiting of Tudor music in the twentieth century by much later English composers like Ralph Vaughan Williams and Michael Tippett.

Music theory

Modernity is marked by a kind of arrogance. What is old, or derives from an earlier age, tends to be relegated to a museum of curios. Nowhere is this more evident than in the realm of technology – notice how funny we find the first attempts to build an aircraft or a submarine or a computer. Mobile phones of just a few years ago strike us as woefully inadequate. There is a tendency for this attitude to begin to dominate our view of the past more generally. The logic of modernity seems to imply that 'everything keeps getting better' even when it quite obviously does not (which is why modernity is also characterized by a sense of 'things aren't what they used to be'). Thinking about old music – or old painting or literature or philosophy – might help remind us that the achievements of the human mind and spirit are not well mapped in terms of an upward moving line on a graph. We might better think in terms of peaks and troughs, waves or cycles, or simply endlessly diverse variations without any particular trajectory towards some final and perfect endpoint.

The smugness of the modern world, applied to music, is partly to do with the technology of modern instruments but it is also to do with the changing sense of what music is and what it is for. Ask anyone on the street: what is music for? The answer is almost always a combination of 'to give pleasure' and 'to express feelings'; it is usually assumed that it does the first by means of the second. But in the centuries before Humanism placed mankind and human emotions at the centre of things (unmarked in music until after about 1550), musicians were often preoccupied by other things. It is not that the medieval musician was uninterested in the realm of human feeling (the intense emotions expressed in songs of courtly love suggest that the yearning love song was as much enjoyed then as now), but that music was conceived of as being something much bigger.

Music in the medieval and Renaissance world, in common with some recent avant-garde music and with many world music traditions, was shaped by a sense of being related to an order of things beyond the everyday ambit of human life. The philosopher Boethius (c.480–524), reiterating a theory first set out by Pythagoras in the sixth century BC, distinguished between three kinds of music. The first, *musica mundana*, was understood as the inaudible harmony of the spheres, the result of the harmonious balance of the cosmos and the movement of the planets within it. *Musica humana* similarly referred to the ideal harmonious balance that held together the world of men. While both these ideas were essentially that – abstract, philosophical ideas – only the third, *musica prattica*, referred to actual music-making as we would recognize it. But this third, practical music, was understood to be an imitation of the first two. In other words, the harmonious combination of sounds in music was not regarded as a self-sufficient phenomenon but as the audible result, in the human sphere, of the larger mathematical and ultimately divine proportions at the heart of the cosmos.

Whereas today we usually think of music in subjective and personal terms, in medieval culture it was allied to scientific thought. In the division of the seven liberal arts (i.e. those things worthy of study by a 'free man') music was grouped not with the arts of communication (the so-called *trivium* of grammar, rhetoric and logic) but with the sciences (the *quadrivium* of arithmetic, geometry, astronomy and music). The idea of music as audible proportion or number, as a kind of sounding mathematics or geometry, continued well into the Renaissance, reflected in theoretical works like the *Proportionale musices* (1476) of Johannes Tinctoris. To be sure, theories of music gradually became less abstract, dealing with practical matters of rhythm, pitch and harmony, but these were still understood in terms of number and proportion, as in the *Instituzioni armoniche* (1558) of Gioseffe Zarlino or the *Dodecachordon* (1547) of Heinrich Glarean.

The interest in number and proportion was not just a theoretical concern but often shaped the way in which composers worked. A cerebral or even mathematical approach to musical composition is often thought to be a phenomenon of modernist music of the twentieth century, but in fact it was a regular conceit of the highly abstract and refined craft of the medieval composer. Consider, for example, the *rondeau* by Guillaume Machaut, 'Ma fin est mon commencement et mon commencement ma fin' (My end is my beginning and my beginning my end). It is written for three voices. The upper voice sings its melody from beginning to end, as one might expect. The middle part, however, sings the same melody backwards – quite literally starting with the last note of the upper voice and working its way back through the entire melody to the first note. At the same time, the lower part forms a palindrome – that is to say, it sings a melodic line up to the halfway point of the song and then sings the same line backwards as the second half of the piece. The basic structure might be represented in words something like this:

Upper voice:	My End Is My Beginning
Middle voice:	Beginning My Is End My
Lower voice:	My End Is My: My Is End My

There would be little remarkable in such a scheme if it resulted in cacophony. The delight of the musician is that such abstract schemes are realized in a completely harmonious interplay of the constituent parts. This play with abstract forms runs through the whole of music history, from Machaut in the fourteenth century to J. S. Bach in the eighteenth century to Arnold Schoenberg in the twentieth. In their '12-note music', Schoenberg and his pupils (Webern and Berg) developed a practice of combining a melodic line with versions of itself played backwards, inverted (or upside-down) and inverted and backwards at the same time. Set against an earlier aesthetic of romantic expression such abstract thinking about music was castigated as a kind of aberration from the true nature of music. It is sobering, then, to think that J. S. Bach had delighted in the same kind of play in his keyboard works, and Machaut, nearly 600 years before Schoenberg, had done much the same.

Notation

These kinds of explorations would not have been possible at all were it not for an increasingly refined system of musical notation. If the history of classical music is essentially the history of *written* music, it is also true that musical techniques and their notation have developed in tandem with each other. Notation did not just record new musical ideas, it made them possible. In the first instance, the notation of the chant melodies was merely an aid to memory. An experienced singer was expected to have memorized thousands of chants, so the earliest forms of notation were ways of prompting the memory as to exactly which chant was to performed. The series of signs, or *neumes*, by which early music was later written down, is thus a very partial set of information. With no staff lines, or staves, precise pitches and intervals could not be specified; instead, the basic contour or outline of each phrase was communicated by a single sign. The term *neume* comes from the Greek word for breath. A *neume* was, in the first instance, a phrase that could be sung in one breath. Later, it came to designate the sign that stood for that phrase. The earliest surviving examples date from the ninth century, though it is likely that the system predates that.

Like so much in the development of music, notation developed in diverse and plural ways according to geographical location. Only gradually did systems develop for the notation of rhythm and only gradually was a system of staves introduced that we recognize today. It was Guido d'Arezzo (*c*.990–1050) who most famously codified the latter (albeit with a 4-line stave as opposed to our modern 5-line version). At first, Guido used colours to indicate which stave line represented which note, but these were later replaced by alphabetic signs to denote the lines for the notes C and F – the origins of our modern clefs (i.e. the 'keys' to which line represented which note). Not only did the lines and spaces represent precise pitches (as they have ever since) but each pitch was given its name. Guido took these from a popular hymn to St John, 'Ut queant laxis', whose first six phrases each began on successive notes of the scale: C D E F G A. He named each of these notes after the syllable of Latin text to which they were set – ut, re, mi, fa, sol, la – names that still survive in the so-called *solfège* system by which many children are taught music.

Rhythmic notation came later; as we have seen, it became increasingly necessary for polyphonic music to find a way to denote rhythm precisely if the different voice parts were to stay together. A complex system of 'ligatures' was developed in the Middle Ages by which pitches were bound into implied rhythmic relations. Though these looked nothing like our modern system of notating rhythm and present a difficult decoding challenge to modern performers and scholars, they were nevertheless an important forerunner of the system we use today. In plainchant, the rhythm in which pitches were sung was shaped by the text; the development of more abstract systems of notating rhythm was thus the necessary precondition of an independent instrumental music, but it also made possible the kind of complex rhythmic play in vocal music from Machaut to Josquin that seems to have nothing to do with the text being set – a play with rhythm for its own sake.

Reformation and Counter-Reformation

By 1600 (which is where chapter 3 takes up the story) the Church no longer exercised such a decisive influence on the development of music. The Age of Humanism, although its impact on music was more belated than in painting and other art forms, opened the way to an idea of music that was more 'modern' in the sense of being shaped around ideas of human expression, entertainment and pleasure. But before that decisive shift the effects of changes in the Church were felt powerfully in the world of music for one last time. The Protestant Reformation, in Germany, France and England, was not only a religious upheaval but a social and political one that dominated much of Europe for centuries to come.

Its effect upon music was perhaps most obviously felt in Germany and France. Martin Luther, whose act of defiance against the Roman Catholic Church in 1517 is generally taken to mark the beginning of the Protestant Reformation, was himself a great music lover, with a special admiration for Josquin. (The more extreme reformer, John Calvin, opposed the use of polyphony in church on the grounds that it obscured the words.) Luther's attitude to music was to promote something in which the congregation could actively participate; the result was what we know today as the hymn – simple strophic religious songs with memorable tunes. Harmonized by the choir, the German chorale came to be a key element of German music for centuries.

In England, sacred music was seriously destabilized by the Reformation from 1534 when Henry VIII broke definitively with Rome. Despite the massive destruction with which the monasteries were suppressed, Henry's own musical taste was conservative and a florid, essentially Latin style of music continued to flourish. Far more destructive to the English musical tradition was the reign of Edward VI (1546–53) in which English musical life was all but destroyed; choral foundations were abolished and many liturgical books burned. Mary Tudor (1553–58) restored the Roman rite, but only for that to be reversed by Elizabeth I (1558–1603). It is an amazing paradox of the age that sixteenth-century English church music shows an astonishing richness notwithstanding all these upheavals of religion and politics. While John Taverner and Thomas Tallis are today the best known of the English choral composers of this age, there were many others who contributed to a musical repertory characterized by a wonderfully rich sound and florid counterpoint – composers like William Mundy, John Shepherd and Christopher Tye.

To some extent, English music was a glorious backwater. In mainland Europe, the Catholic Church responded to the Reformation with the aggressive policies of a Counter-Reformation. For music, the principal effects of this were channelled through the recommendations of the Council of Trent (1545–63); the embodiment of its ideals were found in the Catholic church music of Giovanni Pierluigi da Palestrina (c.1525–94). To this day, Palestrina's style is seen as a model of sixteenth-century modal counterpoint and for centuries was used as an example in teaching. It is an objective, impersonal style, utterly detached from secular concerns, as Palestrina's own life seems to have been. (He lived and worked in the service of the Church in Rome for his whole life.) Musically it is defined by a constant and even flow of well-balanced lines, rising and falling by smooth, stepwise motion. Its moderate and reserved feeling is in marked contrast to the more pointed expression of his contemporary Orlando di Lasso (1532–94), often known simply as Lassus. A far more cosmopolitan and widely travelled composer, Lassus combined Italian and northern musical elements in music in every genre and style – motets, Italian madrigals, French chansons, German Lieder, and Masses. Something of the same heightened feeling is heard in the work of one of the greatest Spanish composers of this age, Tomás Luis de Victoria (1548–1611), but here confined to purely religious genres. In England, the music of William Byrd (1535/40–1623) exemplified the idea of the composer who excelled in every genre, sacred and secular. Byrd wrote Latin Masses and motets, English anthems and services, songs and madrigals, music for viol consort and keyboard instruments.

Looking back over the ground covered by this chapter, it is hard not to be struck by the absolute dominance of vocal music. It is not that instruments had no place in medieval music, both sacred and secular, but their role and status were always separate from that of the voice. All of the most important musical forms were primarily vocal ones. This is in marked contrast to the usual experience of 'classical music' as a primarily instrumental one. To be sure, Mozart or Schubert or Brahms wrote plenty of music for the voice, but from the eighteenth century onwards it is increasingly instrumental music that shapes the key ideas of music history. It is salutary, however, to leave behind the rich colours and dense textures of more recent orchestral and instrumental music to immerse oneself in the clarity of early vocal music. It is hard to avoid the word 'purity'; there is something very honest about a music made up of solo voices in which every sound is exposed and utterly clear. And there is something powerfully intense about the sensuous quality of such pure sounds, reverberating in the empty space of stone buildings. Returning to nineteenth-century orchestral music after drinking such clean, cold water, everything is apt to sound too thickly overlaid and over-flavoured. Nothing can be heard quite as it is for all the excess of activity. Music of the modern age (I include the nineteenth century in this) can sound strangely anxious by comparison, as if it's afraid to stand still or be silent, lest it reveal some underlying absence of voice.

3

Sounding the human: 1600–1750

Dissonance and expression

If today our idea of music is defined in terms of the expression of emotion, then the music of the modern world has its beginning somewhere around 1600. It is not that earlier music was unconcerned with the human, nor that later music ceased to be shaped by religious ideas, but in the decades either side of 1600 a fundamental shift took place in musical language which divides the 'ancient' and the 'modern'. Of course, this did not take place on its own, unrelated to larger changes in European society and culture; it has to be understood as part of the broad current of Humanist thought that defined the emergence of the modern world from the medieval, from the late fourteenth century onwards. At the centre of this great movement of ideas was a massive change in the way in which people saw the world and their own place within it.

It has often been said that medieval painting represents the world as seen through the eyes of God, whereas the new naturalism of the Renaissance represents the world as seen through the eyes of man. This new vision of the world was manifest in specific changes in artistic technique and construction: whereas medieval painting has figures occupying a kind of free-floating, 'non-realistic' space, Renaissance painting is shaped by our modern sense of perspective, a technique which creates the painting in relation to the viewpoint of the individual standing before it. We come to think of this as so self-evident and natural (simply 'the way the world is') that we judge other conceptions in relation to it – whether it be medieval, modern, or non-Western art. The musical equivalent to this shift in visual perspective was a new conception of harmony. Just as perspective intensifies our sense of self-identity, by drawing the world towards a focal point within the individual viewer, so the new harmonic world of music after 1600 has the same effect. This has to do with two related aspects of music: the concept of dissonance, and the sense of musical time.

In layman's terms, the idea of dissonance is something unwelcome in music. Dissonance, by definition, is something ugly and therefore to be avoided since the point of music is to be beautiful, right? Wrong. At least, wrong according to the idea that has shaped almost the entire history of European music. Very little of this music avoids dissonance entirely; music that does, is apt to sound rather bland to our ears. This is because dissonance is the key element in what we usually identify as the expressive quality of music – its 'seasoning' if you like. The reason we find Rachmaninov, or Chopin, or Puccini 'expressive' has a great deal to do with their handling of dissonance.

Whatever their style, all composers from the late fifteenth century to the early twentieth century (and most composers since) have had to reconcile the tension between consonance and dissonance in music. The essence of what we call tonal harmony in Western music is the idea of starting from a keynote and returning to it – the sense of starting out from a stable point (home), diverging to more distant notes (away) and returning (home again). All tonal melodies do this. They don't return straightaway or the melody would be over prematurely; in fact, the expressive quality of a melody is linked directly to how it puts off the sense of closure achieved by a final return to the keynote. A little way in, the melody should feel incomplete, in need of another phrase or two, an effect it achieves by holding off a strong return to the keynote, settling temporarily on other notes instead.

The idea of harmony magnifies this inherent tension in every tonal melody by strengthening both the sense of return, and the sense of incompletion that helps build towards it. The result is a strong sense of movement – away from a starting point and towards some 'necessary' resting point. All these terms are metaphors of course, nothing literally moves, but the effect upon us is powerful and almost physical. This control of movement away from a stable starting point and back to a stable end point is the basic process of all tonal harmony: it shapes every phrase of music, its larger paragraphs and whole sections and movements of a piece. Just as we make sense of writing by following its construction from phrases and sentences, into paragraphs and chapters, so tonal music offers us something similar in terms of the internal divisions created by moments of return to consonant points of rest. Musical forms became longer as composers developed ways of controlling dissonance and resolution on a larger scale. Whereas, in a madrigal written in 1600, dissonance is of the moment and without further consequence, in the early 1700s a composer such as J. S. Bach would build protracted layers of dissonance over many bars in order to intensify the ending of a piece. In a late romantic work, such as Richard Wagner's opera, *Tristan und Isolde* (1859) almost the entire duration of the work (nearly four hours) seems to build up to the long-awaited resolution of the closing bars.

The idea of dissonance, however, is usually understood as a momentary phenomenon – as in a particular chord or sound being dissonant. A basic music theory manual explains how chords are formed, with the building block being the triad, but what it usually omits is that the concept of dissonance is not so much an absolute category as a historically changing one. In medieval organum, as practised by Léonin and Pérotin in the twelfth century, the interval of the third was considered dissonant; the interval at which the melody was doubled was the perfect fourth. To our ears, the fourth sounds bare and nothing like as consonant as the third. In eighteenth-century classical practice, the addition of a seventh to the triad was a carefully calculated dissonant note which set up a powerful 'need' to resolve by means of a cadence. But in Debussy or Dave Brubeck, the addition of the seventh (and indeed other notes of the scale not normally in the triad) sounds perfectly consonant and is not used in a way that requires any resolution.

So why did musical language change in this way? Why was the idea of a modal counterpoint that had served composers for over 300 years thrown over by a new style coming out of Italy around 1600? Such a question brings us right back to key questions of musical meaning and purpose. The short answer is that musical culture shifted from being shaped around the timeless worship of God to the human experience of the here and now. Just as the physical beauty and nobility of the human body were foregrounded in Renaissance sculpture, and a sense of historical time and place enhanced by the new realism in painting, so the new music focused on expressing an immediacy of feeling that seemed to be of the essence of human experience. The timeless world of the medieval modes thus gave way to the directed motion of a new tonal system. The latter's sense of temporal progression and its movement towards clear goals and points of arrival, seemed to express better the spirit of a new mercantile and increasingly dynamic and individualistic age. Nothing reflects this new spirit more than the attitude to musical expression found in the composers of madrigals and early opera in northern Italy around 1600.

Music and the Italian Renaissance

The importance of the new style that emerged in Italy, with its roots in madrigal composition of the later sixteenth century, marks a shift away from the long-standing musical dominance of northern Europe (particularly the composers associated with the Burgundian court). After 1600, Italian composers were at the forefront of European music and exerted a key influence on music in Germany and England. It has often been remarked as odd that Italy should have been pre-eminent in all the arts *except* music for two hundred years earlier, but the reasons for this are tied up with the nature of the Italian Renaissance. The central ideas of that movement were far more amenable to expression in the visual arts and literature than they were in music. The emphasis on realism was founded in depictions of the natural world, of the human body and face, and a focus on individual human experience. Music's distance from the material world (its apparently 'abstract' nature) allied it more readily to the religious and mystical outlook of the medieval world, one that continued well into the sixteenth century. For that reason music produced nothing that paralleled the human drama depicted in the work of Michelangelo (1475–1564), arguably for several centuries.

The secular Humanism of the Italian Renaissance was in part the result of its secular patronage. To be sure, artists and musicians were often in the service of the Pope or his cardinals, but artistic culture was increasingly sponsored by families whose wealth and social status were the result of a powerful mercantile culture – above all, trade and banking. It was for this reason that the Italian cities of Florence, Venice, Milan, Naples, Genoa and Palermo became such important artistic centres, and why such a successful business empire as that of the Medici family found its expression in artistic patronage. Wealth constituted power in this new world, and one of the most powerful embodiments of wealth was art. The richness and extravagance of the new art advertised and celebrated the power and independence of the individual patron and the city-state alike. Florence boasted the talents of artists like Botticelli, Leonardo da Vinci and Raphael, the sculptors Ghiberti and Donatello, and the architect Brunelleschi. Venetian art was defined by the figures of Bellini, Giorgione and Titian.

Towards the end of the sixteenth century, however, music began to discover, in a new sense of harmony and dramatic word setting, something that matched the expressive use of form and colour in Renaissance painting. The gradual emergence of a concern with the emotions expressed in poetry, and the attempt to find musical expression for them, may perhaps be compared with the shift in visual art from the idea of 'God's viewpoint' to a concern with human experience. The vision of the human portrayed by the new music was shaped around feeling: the expression of pain and suffering was the flipside of the highest and noblest sentiments. And it is this, more than anything else, that defined the new era of music.

The label 'baroque', with which historians define the period from *c*.1580 to 1750, is not a very helpful term since it tells us little about the music or how it relates to European society or history more generally. Like the term 'classical' it was coined by a later generation looking back and trying to distinguish their own more modern age from the previous one – in this case, writers in the later eighteenth century who saw the music of their own age characterized by order and clarity. The baroque was understood to refer to the extravagant, unnatural, dissonant, confused and bizarre qualities of a musical style for which intensity of expression, virtuosity and surprise were key. A more helpful way of thinking about this period, from the birth of Claudio Monteverdi (1567) to the death of J. S. Bach (1750) and George Frideric Handel (1759), is that it was defined by a single idea – the representation of the passions or affections. Everything else followed from this, in terms of musical style and forms.

THOROUGHBASS

Technically the music of this period stands out from both earlier and later periods by its use of the so-called *thoroughbass*. Listen to any piece of baroque vocal or instrumental ensemble music and you will hear, strumming along underneath the other parts, one or more instruments not only playing the bass line, but filling out chords above it to provide the harmonic environment which supports the lines above. Around 1600 this was provided by the theorbo or the chitarrone (large lutes), but these were gradually displaced by the harpsichord. You won't hear this in music before 1600 and you won't hear it after about 1770. Around 1600, scores begin to appear consisting of just an upper melody line and an annotated (or 'figured') bass line – the figures being a kind of shorthand directing the keyboard player as to which chords should be played above the bass notes. It signals a loss of interest in the polyphonic part-writing of the sixteenth century and a new primacy of the upper voice.

Words and music: the madrigal

The madrigal is not a form that many of us encounter today. It was essentially a performers' music – a kind of intimate group singing designed for those taking part rather than for an audience. Written generally in four or five parts, it assumed a single solo singer to each part, encouraging far more nuanced expression than could be achieved with a choir. It flourished in Italy (*c*.1550–1620) and England (*c*.1590–1620) but was then overtaken by other forms and interests. I dwell on it here not out of mere historical interest, but because it produced some wonderful and astonishingly powerful music and because it was in this miniature form that so much of the new modern aesthetic of emotional expression was first worked out.

The madrigal's concern with the human rather than the divine was marked outwardly by the fact that it used texts in the vernacular rather than Latin. This was part of a wider movement in which Italian was seen as a worthy language for poetry, an idea fully established in the fourteenth century in the work of Petrarch, Boccaccio and Dante. The term 'madrigal' was originally a poetic one, referring to a form of poetry in which the lines were of irregular lengths. Composers picked up on this aspect and exaggerated it through rapid changes in musical texture. Compared with the constant flow of Renaissance polyphony (exemplified in the music of Palestrina), the sudden changes of texture and technique to reflect changes in the text of the poem seemed modern and shocking to many. The new madrigal highlighted the intensity of each expressive moment, resulting in greater divisions of the musical surface – a series of individual moments in time, held together only by the composer's skill in finding some poetic link between one moment and the next. Where music previously had flowed in long, overlapping lines, the new style was more vertical in its approach. Where continuity and changelessness had been highly valued, the new madrigal style highlighted the opposite – the changeability and mercurial nature of human moods, reflected in dramatic contrasts of texture, harmony and rhythm.

Ironically, the first important madrigal composers were not Italians but drawn from the last generation of 'northern' composers who dominated the musical scene in Italy in the later sixteenth century – men like Adrian Willaert, who published a group of twenty-seven motets and twenty-five madrigals in 1559 under the self-advertising title of *Musica Nova*. The madrigals were mostly settings of sonnets by Petrach and already show a tendency to move between the older style of writing, in relation to the musical dictates of a *cantus firmus*, and the new style of free composition shaped primarily by the words themselves. The single most important forerunner of Monteverdi however was a native Italian composer, Cipriano de Rore, later to be cited as having prepared the ground for the 'second practice', the term by which a new generation of composers working around 1600 distinguished their new style from the old (the 'first practice'). Rore was a pupil of Willaert and succeeded him as *maestro di cappella* at the famous church of St Mark in Venice. He wrote about 100 madrigals, all of them to serious texts in which a new intensity of emotional content was central, drawn out by a new freedom with which harmony was treated. It is here that we find some of the first modern examples of the expressive use of chromaticism – that is, an approach to harmony that uses the semitones either side of the main notes of the scale. Used sparingly, this technique destabilizes the harmony to create passing dissonances for expressive effect; used in a more extreme manner, it begins to undermine any sense of key and thus to create a kind of harmonic 'no-man's-land'.

Inspired by the poetic imagery of the texts they set, madrigal composers moved towards a kind of expressionistic intensity that occasionally threatened the coherence of musical language – the kind of thing one normally associates with musical modernism at the start of the twentieth century, not late sixteenth-century Italian vocal music. The settings of Tasso by Giaches de Wert, who worked for the Gonzaga family in Mantua, provide good examples of this tendency. The effect of the poetry of Torquato Tasso was something like that of the romantic poets two hundred years later. Many madrigal texts were taken from his most famous poems, *La Gerusalemme liberate*, belatedly published in 1580. The cult surrounding his work was only intensified by the fact that he was confined to a mental asylum for eight years in later life. Most famous in this respect is Carlo Gesualdo, whose troubled biography (he murdered his wife in 1590) has been linked to the extreme emotional states of his music in a way that is more normally applied to romantic composers. The polyphonic flow that had guaranteed coherence is here broken up with short-winded musical ideas and overloaded with chromatic detail which, at times, comes close to the breakdown of the musical syntax. Such a style was called 'mannerist' because of its rapid change of musical manner.

Such increasing exaggeration was not sustainable and other madrigalists opted for a rather lighter mood. After Willaert and de Rore the tendency was to set gentle pastoral poems which celebrated innocent rustic delights rather than the urgent emotions of Petrarch. Such works were as easy on the listener's ear as they were on the performer's skill, consisting of singable and memorable tunes expressing gentle emotions. Such an attitude is found in the music of Andrea Gabrieli and Luca Marenzio. The latter was an important influence on the development of the madrigal in England, where this more easy-going aesthetic was the norm. Thomas Morley's madrigals from the 1590s tend towards the pastoral models, often use dance rhythms and retain a simplicity that was directly related to their great popularity, but the more intense expressive language of the Italians also found its way to the English school, as in some of the madrigals of Thomas Weelkes or John Wilbye. A high point of the new expressive style was found in the English 'ayre' or lute song, especially in the work of John Dowland whose intense emotionalism is epitomized in songs like 'Flow, my teares' from his *Second Booke of Songes or Ayres* (1600).

The importance of the madrigal to wider developments in musical language becomes clearest in the several collections published by Monteverdi. His first madrigals were rather old fashioned compared with some of his contemporaries – the *Madrigali spirituali* (1583), *Canzonette* (1584), and Books 1 and 2 of the *Madrigali a 5 voci* (1587 and 1590) were all written while he was still employed in Cremona. He then moved to Mantua, however, where he was employed as part of the musical establishment of the Gonzaga family. His next four sets of madrigals, published between 1592 and 1614, suggest that there he absorbed some of the emotionalism of his predecessor at

Mantua, Giaches de Wert, because these works are altogether darker and more intense in atmosphere.

Books 3 to 6 of Monteverdi's madrigals are dominated by a single topic – erotic love. In this, they are emblematic of a new age in which the refinement of feeling, characteristic of the noble individual, was displayed through a cultivation of the pain and pleasure of love. Monteverdi's music can be taken as the beginning of an idea that shaped music for well over 300 years after him – that musical language offered a uniquely powerful representation of desire. In these madrigals, the sense of unfulfilled yearning was graphically depicted through the spinning out of series of descending sighing lines, pointed at every turn by dissonances between the lines whose 'pain' was precisely the pleasure of the expression – for example, 'Cruda Amarylli' from Book 5, or 'Si ch'io vorrei morire' ('Yes, I would die') from Book 4, which maximizes the sensuousness of musical dissonance to match the erotic content of the poem. The nature of this poetry is demonstrated in the opening lines of 'Luci serene e chiare' from Book 4:

Serene, limpid eyes,
You set me ablaze, yet my heart
Finds pleasure, not pain, in the flames.
Sweet, tender words,
You wound me, yet my breast
Feels no pain, only pleasure.

The conservative reaction to Monteverdi's striking use of harmony was expressed by the theorist Giovanni Maria Artusi who published a tract on 'The imperfections of modern music' in 1600, singling out examples of dissonant harmony in some madrigals by Monteverdi. A riposte, by the composer's brother Giulio Cesare Monteverdi, appeared in the forward to Claudio's *Scherzi musicali* of 1607 in which the departure from older practice was justified by the idea that the new style 'makes the words the mistress of the harmony'. Such disputes between music theorists might seem slightly comic to us now, but they represent the break between two completely different views of what music was about – the unfolding of a purely musical form versus the idea of music in the service of emotional expression.

The birth of opera

The concern with words was not peculiar to composers of madrigals or lute songs nor did it appear out of the blue. In debates about music it took a very particular form. A central tenet of Humanism was the idea of recovering the high culture of ancient Greek and Roman civilizations that, it was considered, had been lost in the Middle Ages. Much ink was spilled in the sixteenth century in theorizing over the relationship of music and words in ancient Greek theatre. That these theories may have had little or no historical truth to them is far less important than the way this activity influenced contemporary thinking about music (not the first or last example of how theorizing is a kind of 'necessary excuse' for taking a new direction in art).

The theorist Girolamo Mei may well have been historically inaccurate in his assertion that tragedy was sung not spoken in ancient Greece, but the idea helped shape a new kind of vocal monody which lay behind the birth of opera around 1600. The importance of this appeal to history was, paradoxically, to show that the recent past was a kind of aberration and thus to legitimate the new as a kind of restoration of something old. This was the gist of Vincenzo Galilei's *Dialogo della musica antica et della musical moderna* (1581), a key text for the influential group clustered around Count Bardi known as the Florentine Camerata. In essence, the polyphonic style was now rejected in favour of a simple, declamatory style of singing in which the clarity of the words, and their musical expression, was everything.

What are generally regarded as the first operas appeared from a rival group gathered around the wealthy nobleman Jacopo Corsi, who presented entertainments at the court of Ferdinand I of Medici. With the poet Ottavio Rinuccini and singer Jacopo Peri, Corsi staged a musical setting in 1597 of an entire dramatic pastoral (the story of *Dafne*) in the new 'stile rappresentativo'. In 1600, the story of *Euridice* was told in the same way, and in 1602 Rinuccini's libretto was set again by the composer Giulio Caccini. These operas were not entirely made up of simple monody – variety was achieved by alternating the solo voice with choral canzonets, madrigals and unison choruses – but the power of narrating a story by means of solo voices was a revelation.

While these first operas may be largely forgotten today, they were shortly followed by Monteverdi's *L'Orfeo* (1607) and *L'Arianna* (1608); the second has been lost, but *Orfeo* survives as the earliest opera still performed today. The Orpheus myth tells the story of Orpheus's journey to the Underworld to rescue his beloved Eurydice from death itself, by charming the gods with the beauty of his music. In the earliest setting of it, as *Euridice* in 1600, the librettist Rinuccini gave the story a happy ending. For Monteverdi's version in 1607, the poet Alessandro Striggio restored the tragic ending by which Orpheus breaks the gods' command not to look back at Eurydice as they exit Hades and thus loses her again to Death. It is hardly coincidental that this story, about the power of music, should have been so central to the development of early opera, nor that Monteverdi's first opera should centre on the same themes of parting and of loss that he had already explored so richly in his madrigals.

While the first operas were the result of the highly theoretical debates of small groups of noblemen, the development of the form quickly became a public concern. It was in Rome that opera really took off as a large-scale and public form – in purpose-built opera houses and staged with elaborate effects, scenery and costumes. The association of opera and grand spectacle was thus established by the middle of the century. In Venice, public opera was more a communal venture by patrician families rather than the product of grand aristocratic wealth. The first opera theatre opened there in 1637, and staged operas by Monteverdi, Cavalli and Cesti. The latter's *Orontea*, performed in 1649, had many repeats over Europe for the next forty years and his model of opera dominated the second half of the century. The refined preferences of the early Florentine camerata for long passages of declamatory recitative now gave way to a popular demand for more melodic arias. The recitative passages thus became progressively shorter, hurried through in order to arrive sooner at the arias. Opera's basic format remained thus for about 200 years until the distinction between recitative and aria was gradually eroded away altogether in the nineteenth century. Of the four operas Monteverdi wrote for this theatre only two survive, *Il Ritorno d'Ulisse in patria* (1641) and *L'Incoronazione di Poppea* (1642).

Though invented in Italy, opera was no less important a form in France, where the distinctiveness of a specifically French opera was fiercely maintained. It is true that the first significant composer of French opera was an Italian – Jean-Baptiste Lully – and that the French court opera cultivated lavish spectacle, but the French theoreticians insisted on the rational element conferred by the words in the face of what they saw as Italian over-emphasis on the music. Lully came to France from Florence at the age of fourteen, as a singer and a dancer, but later worked as a violinist and composer. He became a member of the elite string ensemble, the '24 violons du Roy', at the court of Louis XIV where, from 1653, he was also a composer of instrumental music for the king. In this capacity he collaborated with the great French writers Corneille and Molière in a series of ballet comedies, as well as writing *ballet du cours* – lavish court dances in which the courtiers themselves participated.

Lully's first opera, *Cadmus et Hermione* (1673), was a hybrid work which drew on elements of the French court music tradition, consisting of an overture, followed by grand entry music for the dancers, 'symphonies' to convey action and atmosphere, dances and choruses. The emphasis was on extravagant spectacle and opulence – this was a grand multimedia event of the seventeenth century. From these beginnings developed French opera, known first as *tragédie en musique* and subsequently as *tragédie lyrique*. Though the plot lines were simplified it retained an emphasis on spectacle, magical apparitions and transformation scenes, ballets and characteristic pieces. A good example is *Armide* (1686), an opera that achieved unprecedented success and continued to be reprinted and performed for another century. Unsurprisingly, Lully's immediate successors, André Campra and André-Cardinal Destouches, changed the model very little.

It was perhaps the fixity of the model that ultimately led to a sense of French opera becoming rather formulaic and lifeless. It was largely revived by Jean Philippe Rameau with a string of successful works beginning with *Hippolyte et Aricie* (1733). At first, this opera shocked audiences because of its emotionalism and modern effects of harmony and orchestration and sparked an intense theoretical debate (conducted as a 'war' of polemical pamphlets) about the relative merits of Lully and Rameau. It is a good example of how passionately music has been argued about over the ages and how fiercely change is often resisted. To a later age, it might seem that people argued over relatively small differences in style and technique, but the storms that have raged about music (especially about opera it seems) remind us quite how much music *mattered* to people. Why should people be so affronted by what seems a radical departure in musical style – to the point of rioting in some cases? The answer lies in the

deep-seated relationship between music and the way we experience the world and ourselves. A music that sounds to us to be
irrational or unfeeling or brutal, seems to us to imply a worldview that is irrational or unfeeling or brutal. Worse than that,
because music gets inside us in a way that, say, journalism does
not, music affects us more immediately and powerfully, in both
positive and negative ways.

   In England, as in France, there was initial resistance to opera
as an Italian import. What both these countries had in common
was a very strong tradition of spoken theatre. The English court
had a tradition of masques, involving music, dance and visual
spectacle, comparable in some ways to the French *ballet de cour*.
But the nature of English society and the English court in the
seventeenth century was not conducive to the kind of public
opera that flourished in Italy nor the court opera that flourished
in France. This changed somewhat with the Restoration of the
monarchy in 1660 since Charles II, having spent his exile at the
French court at Versailles, was keen to emulate the French
model. The high points of the English genre are undoubtedly
the dramatic works of Henry Purcell, such as *Dido and Aeneas*
(1689), *King Arthur* (1691) and *The Fairy Queen* (1692). *Dido and
Aeneas*, though a relatively short work, is the only one of his
works to relinquish spoken dialogue completely in favour of
continuous music.

   Despite these national differences, by the early seventeenth
century baroque opera was an increasingly international genre.
The Italian model, based on the alternation of declamatory
recitative and expressive arias, was taken up enthusiastically by
composers all over Europe. The standard form for the aria was
the 'da capo' aria. This consisted of two contrasting sections of
music, but with the first repeated at the end of the second. (The
Italian term 'da capo' meaning, literally, '[go back] to the start'.)
The result is a musical form that can be represented as A–B–A',
one that combines a sense of contrast and dynamic change of

mood with a counterbalancing sense of return and closure. In practice, the repeat of the first section was understood as an opportunity for the singer to ornament the vocal line in order to create a sense of difference in what is otherwise a repeat. This might be done lightly or, in some cases, was taken as an excuse to show off technical brilliance.

The internationalism of the genre is nowhere better demonstrated than in the works of George Frideric Handel, a German composer, working in England but writing Italian operas. His first works were written in Germany in the early years of the eighteenth century where he absorbed Italian influences from composers like Agostino Steffani, then working in Hamburg. But it was in London that Handel was to develop the operatic form, writing around forty operas there between 1711 and 1741, including *Giulio Cesare* (1724) and *Alcina* (1735). The topics of his operas were drawn from Roman history, myth and magic, Persian themes, medieval romance, Renaissance epics and pastorals. Though comic opera was taking off in Italy at exactly the same time, Handel's most successful works tend to be in a more serious, tragic vein.

With the rise of opera as a prestigious and highly cultivated social form of music came the rise of the star performer. A particular kind of male voice, highly prized by opera composers, was the *castrato*. As the name suggests, this was the (unnatural) result of operating on boys before their voices broke in order to preserve the upper register of the voice. Castrato voices were quite different, however, to boys' voices on the one hand and women's voices on the other. The power of this voice-type made it the favoured one for heroic roles, though we know that Handel used women to play male heroes when a castrato was not available. But why write male roles in the upper register at all? The answer lies in the baroque preference for the isolation of the melodic line above the bass – epitomized in the trio sonata, scored typically for two violins and bass, or two flutes and bass. It makes for a curiously powerful kind of interleaving and overlapping that is quite different to the later balance of soprano and tenor voice in the more 'naturalistic' style that took over from the later eighteenth century.

Today, Handel's male roles are either sung by female singers or by counter-tenors (that is, male singers who cultivate a particular kind of upper-register voice). The recent revival in popularity of Handel's operas undoubtedly has much to do with the beautifully sensuous effect of these combinations, of the way in which the intensely rich tone of the counter-tenor blends with the sound of period instruments. Slow, expressive arias in which characters reflect on their predicament, alternate with the swift pace of the action carried by both the recitative and highly energetic orchestral music. But it also has to do with a peculiarly effective balance of the voice and the orchestra. Baroque opera foregrounds and frames the beauty of the voice, something that was often lost in later periods as singers had to contend with bigger orchestras and bigger opera houses. The appetite for powerfully dramatic orchestral effects in nineteenth-century opera brought with it a risk that the singers would be drowned out. To counteract this, singers developed the powerful style of operatic singing we know today – which is why you are unlikely to find the same singer performing both Wagner and Handel.

The sacred concerto, cantata and oratorio

Opera epitomized the Humanist ideal of an art form centred on exploring the range and nature of human experience. But this concern was not confined to secular music; it also had a powerful impact on religious music. Protestantism, with its emphasis on the personal relation between the individual and God, lay behind a baroque tradition of sacred music, especially German sacred music, in which biblical stories were narrated in dramatic form using techniques developed initially in opera. This shift in religious music, to express the human and subjective experience, is marked by the development of the cantata, oratorio and Passion.

The forerunner of these, however, was the sacred concerto developed in Italy in the early seventeenth century. We take for granted now that choral voices can be combined with instruments in big, public works. But the role of instruments in choral music, before about 1600, was almost certainly confined simply to doubling the vocal parts. The change, from simple doubling to a much greater independence of voices and instruments, is marked by a very familiar term – the idea of a *concert*. The Italian verb, *concertare*, means to unite together in harmonious ensemble, translated rather awkwardly into English as 'to concert' or 'to concertize'. The activity, of combining different parts together, produces both the word for an ensemble (a 'concerto' or 'consort') as well as the event at which it plays (a 'concert').

Music that combined many parts, vocal and instrumental, independent but bound together, expressed an ideal of social cohesion and power. The development of the *concertato* style is often linked to the cathedral of St Mark in Venice where both the acoustic and the architecture suggested the kind of alternating 'choirs' of instruments and voices explored in the music of Giovanni Gabrieli, notably in the *Sacrae symphoniae*, Book 1 of which was published in 1597, and Book 2 in 1615. But the new *concertato* style perhaps had far more to do with Venice as a centre of the new urban, mercantile world defined by the need to establish harmony between different parts on a grand scale. For the listener, there was nothing abstract about this idea: the experience of these big dramatic polychoral works would have afforded a visceral thrill of contrasts and juxtapositions.

Claudio Monteverdi, dismissed from the service of the Duke of Mantua in 1612, was appointed the following year as *maestro di capella* at St Mark's in Venice, a post he held for the next thirty years. There he pioneered a kind of dramatic large-scale choral music with instruments, written for the Doge and the Senate but clearly intended as public works. This is a long way from the devotional religious music of earlier centuries made 'for the glory of God' alone, irrespective of whether anyone but the performers were present to hear it. A work like Monteverdi's *Vespro della beate Vergine* (1610), written while he was still working in Mantua but published in Venice, may well have been a way of advertising his ability to write in the monumen-tal, polychoral style. It is a work that calls out for a large perfor-mance space and an audience to witness it.

Outside of St Mark's, the development of non-operatic vocal and choral music was rather more modest. The cantata and sacred concerto were the result of exploiting the expressive devices of early opera without the need for (often prohibitively) expensive staging. Like the opera, these forms employed an alternation of recitative and aria combined to narrate a single dramatic story. Typically for one or two solo voices (possibly three), 'in concert' with an instrumental basso continuo group, they were as much an outgrowth of the madrigal as the opera, but allowed a greater focus on the single monodic line against a harmonic bass. Though the term 'cantata' is today more often associated with sacred texts, the early cantata was just as likely to be on secular themes, setting texts rather like those of earlier madrigals. It is a form that has survived less well than both the madrigal and opera – few of the 300 extant cantatas of Luigi Rossi, for example, are heard today, nor those of Giacomo Carissimi or Antonio Cesti.

In Germany the sacred concerto flourished but with a distinctive and central addition – the Lutheran chorale. Developed in the vast output of Michael Praetorius, the German choral tradition produced a huge flowering of music, a century before the choral music of J. S. Bach, in the works of Johann

Schein, Samuel Scheidt and Heinrich Schütz. The latter had been a pupil of Gabrieli in Venice, and later had contact with Monteverdi. His absorption of the Italian style is obvious in his own grand concertato works for two or more choirs such as the *Psalmen Davids* (1619) and *Symphoniae sacrae* (1629).

As was the case in opera, choral music both exhibited some clear national characteristics and was a medium for mixing them up and crossing national boundaries. While Europe was ravished by the Thirty Years War (1618–48), originally a dispute between German Protestants and Catholics but which widened into a much wider national conflict, musicians freely mixed the French, Italian and German idioms. The startling contrasts of colour achieved in the polychoral works of Venetian composers were combined with the intense dramatic expression of monody developed in Florentine opera. The sober nature of German religious choral music came into contact with the high emotional temperature of the Italian *concertato* style, itself contrasted to the simplicity of secular German song.

Music in England largely resisted foreign influences. Following the execution of Charles I, the Commonwealth (1649–60) was characterized by a puritannical suspicion and indeed hostility towards music that resulted in the institutions of English church music being disbanded and closed down altogether – a destructive act from which they never really recovered. At the Restoration of the monarchy in 1660, King Charles II brought with him a preference for French music, having spent part of his exile at the court of Versailles. Nevertheless, English church music persisted and even flourished in the setting of texts drawn from the Book of Common Prayer (1549) as anthems – both the verse anthem (which alternated solo verses with choral ones) and the full anthem (a choral motet). The best-known composer of these is undoubtedly Henry Purcell, who wrote more than sixty, but the form was developed in important ways by his immediate predecessors Pelham Humfrey and John Blow.

If the anthem defines English choral music of the seventeenth century, the following century was to be defined by the oratorio, above all as developed by Handel. The oratorio is essentially the telling of a biblical story, but one that draws out the human drama of the story by recourse to the musical devices refined in opera – recitative, aria and dramatic chorus. In many ways the oratorio was to the eighteenth-century audience what the Hollywood religious epic was to the twentieth, or the vast biblical scenes of Renaissance painters were to the sixteenth century. It was the situation of the human characters in these stories that was to be drawn out – their emotions and passions. Perfected by Handel in works from *Esther* (1732) to *Jeptha* (1752), the genre includes one of the most famous classical works of all time, the *Messiah* (1741). This most English of forms was still being practised by Mendelssohn in the nineteenth century, in works like *St Paul* (1836) and *Elijah* (1846) and by English composers well into the twentieth century, such as William Walton's *Belshazzar's Feast* (1931).

While Handel's vocal and choral music is best defined through his operas and oratorios, that of his contemporary Johann Sebastian Bach (1685–1750) is exemplified in the cantata and Passion. Bach's career can be divided according to the three principal positions he held during his lifetime: from 1708 to 1717 he was court organist at Weimar; from 1717 to 1723 he was music director to Prince Leopold of Anhalt at Cöthen; and from 1723 to 1750 he was cantor of St Thomas Church and director of music for the city of Leipzig. These three quite different situations necessarily shaped the kinds of music he wrote. Many of his organ and keyboard works date from the first period, his chamber and orchestral works from the second, and most of his cantatas from the third. For almost two years, while he was at Leipzig, Bach wrote a new cantata every week, to be performed as part of regular Sunday worship as well as for the feast days of the Church year. Nearly 200 such works survive, though it is likely that he wrote far more.

Because of their origin in weekly worship, sung after the reading of the Gospel and before the sermon, Bach's cantatas are necessarily relatively small-scale in terms of their vocal and instrumental forces. They are sectional pieces and therefore flexible in duration. The combination of chorus, solo arias, recitatives and instrumental music allows for a variety of different modes of speech. The framing function of the outer movements, carried by the chorus, is often richly layered, perhaps fugal, and festive in character – as, for example, in 'Ein feste Burg ist unser Gott' (BWV 80). The inner movements typically alternate between narrative and contemplative modes, i.e. recitatives and solo arias or duets. In the arias, the voice often interacts with a solo instrumental *obbligato* (perhaps a flute, oboe or solo violin) that, in imitation of the vocal part, fills the gaps between the phrases of the voice. A key element of the cantata, generally appearing in the outer sections, is the chorale – the simple hymn in which the congregation would have joined with the choir in singing.

On a far larger scale are Bach's settings of the Passion story and the Mass. Two Passions survive, the *St John Passion* (1724) and the *St Matthew Passion* (1727), extended works in the style of the oratorio but distinguished by the particular story that they narrate. Bach's massive B minor Mass remains something of a mystery. It was assembled by Bach in 1749, shortly before his death, from sections of music he had written over the previous twenty-five years. Its huge scale (nearly two hours in duration) suggests it was not intended for liturgical use, and the fact that Bach, a Lutheran, set the Catholic Latin mass has perplexed scholars ever since. All Bach's music, no matter how functional, was written 'to the glory of God', but this work, it seems, had no other function. It remains one of the most astonishing

documents of classical music, not just as a summation of the
compositional skill Bach had acquired over a lifetime and thus as
a highpoint of baroque music, but as a sustained meditation on
the divine with few parallels in Western culture.

The rise of instrumental music

Our notion of classical music is dominated by instrumental
music – the orchestra, the piano, the string quartet. The primacy
of the voice before the seventeenth century is therefore very
striking. Of course, instruments had existed in Europe for
thousands of years, but instrumental music was generally not
accorded the same status as music for the human voice. This is
underlined by the fact that a good deal of the music played on
instruments was originally written for voice. The change in the
status of instrumental music is also part of the Humanist
Renaissance: it has to do with the idea of a self-sufficient music
whose only purpose was pleasure, outside of any religious
function and thus not tied to any words. With the establishing
of commercial music publishing in Italy and France, secular
instrumental music began to gain a stronger presence. There was
a sudden outpouring of music for the lute, for example, after
about 1540, and a corresponding appearance of music for
keyboard instruments and instrumental ensembles. In England,
the collection of keyboard music known as the *Fitzwilliam
Virginal Book* (1609–19) brought together pieces from many of
the leading composers of the day. (The virginal was a small
keyboard instrument.)

Instrumental music before this time was largely tied to dance
forms and a key genre, particularly for keyboard music, thus
became sets of variations written on dance tunes. Leading dances
of this time were *pavanes* (in slow duple time) and *galliards* (in fast
triple time). Such dances form the basis of extended and

complex elaborations in pieces by English composers such as William Byrd and John Bull, found in the *Fitzwilliam Virginal Book*. The regularity of dance both made possible and provoked a kind of improvisatory variation, allowing musicians to engage in virtuoso departures from the melody without disturbing the underlying framework of the piece. This was almost certainly the practice in live performance (if only to offset the performers' boredom at having to repeat the same passage over and again), and composers took this as a starting point in writing more formal variations. This is one of the most enduring of compositional principles, based on preserving some essential attributes of a melodic or harmonic passage but freely altering others. This often consists of an increasingly complex kind of ornamentation or decoration of the theme but, in more extended sets, can result in variations that are completely different in character from the opening material.

Thomas Morley, one of the chief exponents of the new keyboard music as of the English madrigal, described the keyboard fantasia thus in his *Plain and Easy Introduction to Practical Music* (1597): 'The most principal and chiefest kind of music which is made without a ditty is the fantasy, that is, when a musician taketh a point at his pleasure and wresteth and turneth it as he list making either much or little of it as shall seem best in his own conceit. In this may more art be shown than in other music, because the composer is tied to nothing but that he may add, diminish and alter at his pleasure.' This is an important statement of the self-sufficiency of musical invention and, indeed, musical pleasure. The idea of a composer's freedom to invent wherever the mood takes him, tied to neither text nor prescribed form, marks out this attitude to music as quite new.

In France, keyboard music of the seventeenth century inherited and transformed the rich literature of lute music. As with English keyboard music, this often meant taking simple dance pieces and elaborating upon them. French pieces typically present the dance in its simple form and then again, as a 'double', with the addition of carefully judged ornamentation. It was not only the repertoire of the lutenists that was copied (dances, preludes, tombeaux and character pieces) but also the style of playing too. The so-called *style brisé* (or 'broken style') imitates on the keyboard what was a necessity on the lute – the spreading of a chord in a sequence of notes in order to sustain the volume of sound. For a while then, keyboard composers and players rather neglected the possibilities of their instrument. This changed in the music of Jacques Champion de Chambonnières, who is regarded as having founded the French *clavecin* school.

François Couperin may be said to embody the spirit of French keyboard music and its aesthetic. He published his pieces in twenty-seven *ordres*, collected into four *livres*. Each *ordre* consists of a set of pieces, as with the German suite, but we do not know whether they were to be played in a set order without omissions (as we believe was the case for the suite). That these pieces appear to be for the pleasure of the players – not concert pieces in a modern sense – the likelihood is that one could play as many or as few as one wished, and in any order. All the pieces have elaborate titles – referring to different dance types, characters, moods, events and real people – but the link between the music and the title is far more allusive than we might assume today (this is, after all, a century or more before the idea of 'programme music' developed). The German equivalent was the keyboard suite – a set of dances in the same key, which typically included the courante, allemande, sarabande, gigue and minuet. Bach's sets of six French suites, six English suites and six partitas (effectively, German suites) represent a high point of a tradition which stretches back to the early seventeenth century.

String music

It was at this time that the instruments of the modern violin family rose to the central position that they still hold in classical instrumental music. The violin first appears in European music, early in the sixteenth century, as a *viole da braccio* as opposed to a *viole da gamba* (that is to say, 'of the arms' rather than 'of the legs'), being thus distinguished from what we now refer to simply as the viol. There were other differences too – unlike the *viole da gamba* the *viole da braccio* was unfretted (a guitar has frets along its fingerboard, a violin does not) and bowed with an overhand grip. The latter meant that a firmer pressure could be applied to the instrument, thus allowing the strings to be held in a tighter tension and so producing a louder, more clearly defined sound quality. The violin was thus gradually associated with a music characterized by sharper attacks, more emphatic rhythms and less flowing lines. Lest these all sound like gains, they come of course at the price of corresponding losses – the loss of the softer, more blended tone of the viol. Listening to the

THE VIOLIN

The high point of the violin's development took place in Italy in the late seventeenth century and early eighteenth. Specifically, it centred on one city, Cremona, and the work of a few master craftsmen: Antonio Stradivari, Nicolo Amati and several members of the Guarneri family. Violins made from their workshops are still regarded today as the best in the world and, when they sell, fetch huge prices. At a public auction in 2006, a Stradivarius violin went to an anonymous bidder for $3,544,000. Nobody is entirely sure where their highly prized tone comes from – theories include the idea that it is due to the kind of wood they are made from or even the chemicals used to treat the wood.

sumptuous sound and flowing part-writing of Purcell's music for viol consort (the *Sonatas*, *Fantasies* and *In Nomines*) brings home at once what was sacrificed in the development of the modern string quartet.

In the first instance, a good violinist or cellist should be able to make their instrument sing like the human voice. Fundamentally, all instrumental music started from this instinct, to imitate the expressive tone and gesture of the voice. But it was just a starting point; the attraction of the new instrumental music was that it could also 'take off' from this origin, to elaborate a musical world that the voice could not, as when a violinist presents a simple melody but then opens it out in a set of increasingly virtuoso variations, as in the massive Chaconne in D minor for solo violin by J. S. Bach.

Unsurprisingly, music for violins was initially developed in northern Italy, in sonatas for one or two violins (with basso continuo) and later in concertos for one or more instruments and string orchestra. While the concerti of Antonio Vivaldi are today the most famous (he wrote over five hundred concerti, including works for many other instruments), his model of the concerto was indebted to the earlier works of Arcangelo Corelli, Giuseppe Torelli and Tommaso Albinoni. While the solo sonata or trio sonata (actually for two solo instruments and basso continuo) was essentially a small-scale kind of instrumental music for relatively intimate performance, the concerto grew into an instrumental form that eventually matched the drama of the opera and large-scale choral works. In the larger musical institutions (such as those at court), groups of string players were differentiated into 'rank and file' players who would have doubled the vocal parts, and virtuoso solo players who played contrasting solo sections – as, for example, in sacred concertos. In the vocal works of Alessandro Stradella, for example, the instruments are divided into a solo *concertino* group and a larger, *concerto grosso*. This division, reproduced in purely instrumental works as a solo instrument and a *ripieno* group, is the basis of the concerto format as we still know it today.

By 1700, in the work of Corelli and Torelli, the string concerto assumed its typical three movement form (fast-slow-fast) in which a soloist (or pair of soloists) alternates with returns of the ensemble. Between these *ritornello* sections, the soloist takes flight in more virtuosic passagework, generally aligned to harmonic modulation and thus a sense of movement (with the *ritornello* sections confirming the new key, or return to the original one). A sense of great energy and dynamism is key to the outer movements of the concerto, while the slow central movement typically draws on the expressive singing quality of the solo instrument. Taken as a whole, the baroque concerto balanced mechanical brilliance and affective pathos. The clarity of exchange and contrast between the soloist and ensemble, the constant repetition of the ritornello theme, the driving rhythms and clear harmonic structure, all contributed to a style that ensured an immediate and powerful impact upon the listener – still as strong today as it was in the early 1700s, judging by the continued popularity of the baroque concerto. Its influence spread quickly from northern Italy to Germany and to England, shaping the concertos of Telemann, J. S. Bach and Handel. Bach made several arrangements of Vivaldi violin concertos for keyboard (both organ and harpsichord) and his larger debts to Vivaldi shape his own rich contributions to the form – the six Brandenburg Concertos of 1721.

There is no contradiction in the fact that the rise of instrumental music, particularly that associated with the violin family, grew out of the expressive concerns of the composers of early madrigals and opera. It was only in a much later age that instrumental music was discussed as 'abstract' and wrapped up entirely in its own technical aspects, as if it were unconcerned with human feeling. It is quite clear that composers of string music and keyboard music often imitated the expressive quality of vocal music, transposing into instrumental music a rich vocabulary of emotional 'affects' without these being tied to any particular idea or poetic content. But the rise in instrumental music was also a product of another aspect of the Humanist insistence on the world of man, an exploration of what it was to be human. Instrumental music became a modern expression of that concern with the nature of human life. This is true superficially, in the increased emphasis placed upon music as a secular pleasure, an entertaining and pleasurable pastime for its own sake. But it is also true in a deeper way, in that the medium of instrumental music was increasingly understood as a vehicle for exploring and expressing a sense of individual and collective experience. It was this idea, more than any other, that accounts for the huge value attached to music by the beginning of the nineteenth century.

4
The classical ideal: 1750–1810

The classical style

The idea of a classical style implies a set of 'timeless' values: order, balance, harmony, restraint, elegance, beauty. So how did it happen that the music of only three composers (Haydn, Mozart and Beethoven) working largely in a single European city (Vienna) over a period of no more than forty years (c.1770–1810) came to define, almost exclusively, our notion of musical classicism? The answer is partly that, like most historical terms, the label 'classical' was not applied to music until after the period itself was over. The term appears from about 1830 in the writings of historians and music theorists who used it to distinguish their own age by means of its contrast with an earlier one. Because romanticism was understood in terms of individualism and deviation from received musical forms and styles, the period immediately before it was retrospectively constructed as its opposite – as a time in which formal models and musical conventions were brought to a kind of perfection. Stylistic practices established in the late eighteenth century, no less historical and changeable than any other period in the history of music, were thus dubbed 'classical' as a way of defining a later, more modern age, self-conscious about its own historical difference. But the idea has stuck and been remarkably powerful ever since; until quite recently, the history of music was told as a story that 'leads up' to the classical era, whereby the classical style represents an ideal against which the more recent past (i.e. music after Beethoven) is defined either by conservative imitation or by progressive deviation and experiment.

Today, the classical style is recognized both by its key musical genres – string quartet, solo sonata, symphony and concerto – and by characteristic aspects of musical language, such as its well-balanced symmetrical melodies and its clear sense of musical direction and form. Key to the classical style is the idea of balance as the basis of musical beauty. Not only should the phrases of a single melody be balanced, but also the different sections of a piece. That said, the classical style does not shy away from contradictory elements; though it is often thought of in terms of restraint and a rather formal manner, it can also be highly dramatic and emotionally unpredictable. What defines the classical style is not the absence of these elements but a way of holding them in equilibrium. The slow movement of a Mozart concerto might be deeply introspective and subjective, but the finale restores a sense of breezy lightness and collective celebration. A harmonic progression might appear to take an unexpected turn that leads the music off in a new direction, but the larger phrase structure later makes sense of this and returns us to familiar ground.

Thinking about such stylistic and aesthetic ideals is a more useful way to characterize a particular musical period than worrying too much about dates. The span of forty years between 1770 and 1810 is as good as any for delimiting the high classical period: 1770 was the year of Beethoven's birth and 1810 the year after Haydn's death. More importantly perhaps, the 1770s are often taken as the beginning of a new style of composing that emerged in the work of Haydn and Mozart, while by 1810 Beethoven had completed all the major works of his so-called middle period. In the following decade not only did Beethoven's own style change significantly, but the work of younger composers – Weber, Rossini, Schubert – was already taking music in quite different musical directions.

Of course, stating where one style period ends and another begins is as impossible as judging where a river ends and the sea begins. The principal elements of the classical style were already evident in music by 1750, the year in which Johann Sebastian Bach died. His death at the century's midpoint might be taken, symbolically at least, as a definitive end of a baroque era that was already giving way to a quite different conception of music. The new stylistic directions can be neatly represented by Bach's own sons, notably Johann Christian Bach and Carl Philipp Emanuel Bach, but the generational divide of father and sons marks a bigger historical divide. To the younger generation, the 'old' style of the baroque was unappealingly serious and complex. It survived through the eighteenth century as the 'learned style', self-consciously conservative and appreciated only by the musical connoisseur. It was displaced by something more immediately pleasurable and entertaining. In his highly influential treatise, *On the True Art of Keyboard Playing* (1753), C. P. E. Bach distinguished between these as the 'learned' and the 'galant' styles. Where the 'learned' was complex, abstract and rather cerebral, the 'galant' was characterized by its appealing simplicity.

The difference can be heard at once by comparing a fugue by Johann Sebastian Bach with a simple sonata movement by his son, Johann Christian. The comparison is rather like that between, on the one hand, a complex debate involving several people, all of whom talk at the same time without pausing for breath, sometimes mumbling, sometimes arguing rather stridently, and, on the other hand, a simple story, delivered by a single expressive speaker in short, clear sentences. It is not only that the baroque texture is contrapuntal (two or more voices working 'against' each other) but also that the music seems to spin out in great arching cycles without obvious points of rest. By contrast, the early classical textures of the 'galant' style consist of short phrases punctuated by simple cadences. A single melodic line, usually in an upper voice (e.g. soprano, violin or upper register of the keyboard) was typically supported by the other voices in an accompanying role (e.g. simple chords or broken arpeggios in the lower part of the keyboard, or the remaining instruments of a string quartet).

The opening sections of classical pieces are easily recognized by the symmetry of their musical phrases. Almost any movement by Haydn or Mozart will provide an example of this. A simple melodic idea is stated which seems to fall into two parts, rather like a question and answer, with a clear moment of punctuation between them, and with the second somehow completing the first. It is the musical equivalent of a simple rhyming scheme in poetry that 'makes sense' rhythmically even when the words don't. Musical phrases do not literally rhyme but they create a similar effect, partly through the repetition of rhythmic patterns and partly through a sense of question and answer that derives from the opposition of simple harmonic progressions. The midpoint of a phrase thus comes to a temporary rest but seems to require some answering phrase in order to close fully. Just as you can reduce a verse of poetry to its underlying structure of rhyme and rhythm by means of nonsense syllables and the poem still make 'musical' sense, so too, you can reduce the opening of most classical movements into patterns that make sense simply in terms of the rhythm of their constituent phrases. Try it with the opening of a Haydn String Quartet or a Mozart Piano Sonata.

Music and the Enlightenment

Such changes in musical style do not happen in a vacuum. To understand what classical music *is* one has to ask far more than *how* or *when* music changed – one has to ask *why*, *where* and *for whom* it changed. The classical style marks a very particular moment not only in music history but in the history of

European culture more generally. It signalled a new sensibility, a new way of experiencing oneself and the wider world, and, in doing so, it underlined the ways in which the world itself had changed. It is rare for music to engage directly with the world of politics, economics or philosophy, but the social changes registered and shaped in these areas of life are also active, below the surface, in the development of music. Music may not show any obvious relationship to the kind of philosophical and political thinking that lay behind the huge current of social change in the eighteenth century, but it nevertheless articulated a new way of feeling that was part of that change.

Key to the 'Age of Reason' were the English empirical philosophers, Edmund Burke, John Locke and David Hume, who insisted that received ideas of the world should be tested by logical thought applied to the evidence of the senses. This was far more than an abstract, philosophical matter. These were also men of action, statesmen and reformers, who applied their thinking to real social and political issues. So too, the French 'philosophes' like Voltaire, Denis Diderot, Montesquieu and Jean-Jacques Rousseau, used the idea of reason to attack not just superstition and irrationality but the social hypocrisy and privilege built upon it. Their writing helped provoke all kinds of social reforms, at the heart of which were the 'inviolable' rights of the individual. Enlightenment thought thus had very practical and far-reaching consequences, especially when its principles were taken up by Europe's most powerful monarchs – like the Habsburg emperor Joseph II or his mother Maria-Theresa. A new conception of the individual lay directly behind the abolition of serfdom and slavery, and the move towards democracy and self-determination signalled by the American Revolution (1776) and the French Revolution (1789). All the political and economic rights of the individual that we take for granted in a modern democratic society were definitively marked out during this period.

While philosophers or political theorists wrote about the rights of the individual, artists and musicians provided ways to express such claims in terms of feeling. The modern individual was thus characterized by 'sensibility', in the sense Jane Austen later captured in her novel *Sense and Sensibility* (1811). Indeed, the eighteenth-century novel was perhaps the single most important vehicle for this heightened awareness of the emotional inner life of the individual. It was, moreover, no longer concerned with the emotions of mythic heroes and heroines or grand historical figures, but the feelings of ordinary people living outwardly ordinary lives. Early milestones of this movement include Samuel Richardson's novels *Pamela, or Virtue Rewarded* (1740) and *Clarissa* (1748); Samuel Johnson praised the latter for being 'the first book in the world for the knowledge it displays of the human heart'. It is against this backdrop that one can understand the move to a new, simpler style in music. The emphasis was on the arousal of 'natural feeling' – unaffected and sincere emotions which, it was believed, offered a better guide to right and moral action than the obscure abstract systems of baroque thought.

But if music was shaped by the rationalism of the eighteenth century (evident in the new order and 'grammar' of its musical materials) it was also an ideal vehicle for the anti-rational reactions of the later part of the century. The *Sturm und Drang* was a movement in German literature that emphasized the irrational element of feeling. One of its key works is undoubtedly Goethe's novel *The Sorrows of Young Werther* (1773), a story of unrequited love and eventual suicide that acquired cult status (and apparently led to the tragic deaths of many real-life lovers who chose to emulate their fictional hero). The power of disorder in nature was frequently represented in paintings – shipwrecks and storms were a favourite subject matter, as in the work of Claude-Joseph Vernet (e.g. *Shipwreck* of 1759) or Phillipe-Jacques Loutherbourg (e.g. *Defeat of the Spanish Armada*, 1796). The musical equivalent can be found in some of the minor key symphonies of Mozart and Haydn. A sense of instability and agitation was created by syncopated rhythms, chromatic harmony, string tremolandi, unusual orchestration and wide melodic leaps. The effect is of something thrilling rather than unpleasant – like watching a storm from the safety of your home. The first movement of Mozart's Symphony No. 25 in G minor, K.183 (1773), provides a good example.

In some ways, a tendency to drama was built into classical music. Whereas baroque pieces generally demonstrate what was known as a 'unity of affect' (i.e. a single idea or emotion), composers of the classical period were much more concerned with contrasting quite different emotional states within the same piece. This is a structural feature of one of the most important musical forms of the age – the sonata form. Just as poetry has its different forms – the ode, the elegy, the ballad, the sonnet – so too does music. The sonata form has something in common with the dramatic ballad or epic, in that it unfolds like a drama or story; of course, instrumental music does not literally tell a story, but in sonata form it carries on *as if* it did. Purists might disapprove of the once popular habit of making up storylines to Beethoven sonatas, and perhaps Beethoven himself might have disapproved, but the music not only lends itself to such a gloss, it practically encourages it. The classical sonata presents musical characters, often sharply contrasted, which recur throughout the movement in different guises and moods. They appear to be the agents of the dramatic action of the music, just as things appear to happen to them. It seems to be the musical characters themselves that suffer, fight, triumph or play.

Patronage

The musical effects of the social changes brought about by the Enlightenment were undoubtedly marked by changes in style, but it was in the outward life of music that the change was most obviously seen. The shift from an idea of the musician as a retained servant in the pay of an aristocratic or ecclesiastical patron, to the more modern idea of the independent artist, free to create whatever his artistic imagination dictated, is a defining marker of the modern age. J. S. Bach spent his working life in the service either of wealthy patrons or the church; Joseph Haydn spent most of his working life in the service of Prince Nicholas of Esterházy before his success as a composer and income from the publication of his works allowed him to become independent. Ludwig van Beethoven famously defended his freedom to compose what he wished, but was nevertheless supported financially by a consortium of wealthy aristocrats. Their willingness to do so, based on a faith in the absolute value of great art rather than any immediate purpose, became a model for modern patronage (whether by the state via organizations like the Arts Council or from charitable foundations and private individuals).

The very different lives of these three composers underlines the profound change, within a single century, from an idea of music shaped by its function in religious worship or as aristocratic entertainment, to the idea of an art music, free from any external function, that continues to underpin our idea of classical music today. It provides a concrete demonstration of some of the social changes brought about by the Enlightenment. The shift of weight from ecclesiastical authority to secular thinking and institutions was a gradual one; composers and musicians continued to be employed by the church throughout the nineteenth and twentieth centuries but, with a few exceptions, the key figures in the new musical styles identified themselves with secular instrumental music. The waning of aristocratic patronage was rather more dramatic. Though Wagner still depended on the financial support of King Ludwig II of Bavaria in the 1860s and composers like Stravinsky still accepted commissions from wealthy individuals in the early twentieth century, Haydn was the last composer of major significance to be employed as retained 'staff' in the service of a wealthy aristocratic family. The familiar picture of Beethoven as archetypal genius – all wild hair and fierce independence – has to be offset against the image of Haydn dressed in the servant's livery of the Esterházy family and producing music to order for their entertainment. That Mozart died penniless and was buried in a pauper's grave is more than the stuff of Hollywood films; it reflects the very real economic precariousness of the composer suddenly at the whim of the marketplace.

Mozart's story is symptomatic of the new age. Originally in the service of the Archduke of Salzburg, he resigned his position in 1781 to go to Vienna and make his way as an independent performer and composer. A decade later he was dead, aged only thirty-five, having experienced both huge success and great struggle for survival. His audience was a mixed one, and the diversity of Mozart's output reflects the different demands and tastes of the Viennese public. Music for the Church was one thing, for the opera house quite another. Mozart's piano sonatas reflect the economic importance of teaching private and wealthy piano pupils and the market for music publishing; his concertos and symphonies reflect the growth of public concerts for a paying audience.

The growth of a middle-class audience for music was itself a product of the Enlightenment; the corollary of curbing the power of the aristocracy was that the pleasures formerly enjoyed exclusively by a wealthy minority were increasingly opened up to a wider section of society. In fact, the concert hall and opera house were important sites for the mixing of different strata of society. Mozart's world was a very hierarchical one, but it was also a dynamic one in which music was an ideal way of moving between different social 'levels' (as his father once reminded him in a letter, advising him always to make sure he wore a decent wig and plenty of rings, so as to make a good impression).

The new audiences for music were reflected in new genres of music. The massive growth in keyboard music in the eighteenth century followed the burgeoning interest in domestic music making, which first the clavichord and then the new fortepiano (antecedent of the modern piano) made possible in many private homes. Similarly, the central place of chamber music (particularly the string quartet) in classical music reflects the importance not just of concerts but also of amateur music making and private salons. In the early nineteenth century, the development of the Lied (German art song) was similarly shaped by domestic music making. The classical symphony, concerto and overture are unthinkable without the institutions of the concert hall and its audience, but also of a new *attitude* to music that transformed it into an object of passive contemplation and appreciation. The massive rise of instrumental music was made possible by new technologies of instrument production and the growth of new ensembles (above all the symphony orchestra), but it was the new *idea* of music, as a meaningful, expressive language, that drove all of these changes.

When we talk of the classical era we are very often talking specifically of *Viennese* classicism. It is not that these changes did not take place elsewhere (London, Paris, Naples, Berlin, Mannheim, Prague and other cities were all important centres) nor that there were not important composers working elsewhere (J. C. Bach, C. P. E. Bach, Sammartini, Stamitz, Graun), but that Vienna became the undisputed centre of the new style, and Mozart, Haydn and Beethoven its undisputed representatives. Historians remind us that the music of this triumvirate grew from a hinterland of less well-remembered composers (Salieri, Wagenseil, Dittersdorf, Vanhal, Cimarosa) who all shared a common musical language, and that at Beethoven's death in 1827 the biggest musical name in Europe was that of Rossini. But our fixation on Haydn, Mozart and Beethoven shows little sign of abating, and the ideal of music that they are seen to represent still largely defines our sense of what classical music is.

Opera

Nowhere does music connect more directly to the realities of social life than in opera. For all its obvious absurdity, compared with the abstract business of instrumental music, opera at least represents human characters in dramatic interaction. Though the level of stylization involved in having people sing rather than speak might be thought to count opera out from any claim to realism, its power clearly derives directly from the intensity with which music vivifies the emotions of the characters. This, more than anything else, distinguished it from spoken drama. The attraction of opera, from the works of Monteverdi onwards, lay in its balancing of the representation of public interaction (the dramatic situations of the characters on stage) and private feeling (the musical expression epitomised in the aria). Opera's importance to Western culture derives in part from this productive tension. The necessity of balancing outward statement and action with inward feeling and thought was part of modern life; at the opera one could empathetically suffer and rejoice with the characters, without having to suffer any real-life consequences.

In the classical era, opera became a powerful vehicle for representing the changed social status of ordinary people. In the baroque, opera had frequently functioned as a symbolic representation of the authority of the monarch: in the court of Louis XIV, for example, mythic stories of the gods were understood to refer back to the king himself. But the eighteenth century saw an increasing focus on 'ordinary people', the dramas of their lives and feelings. Indeed, the gap between different social strata was often the basis of comic opera. The drama on stage was all the more pointed given the mixed nature of the opera audience, barely separated by the symbolic and physical space of the auditorium itself (stalls, upper and lower circles, boxes, amphitheatre).

The changing nature of eighteenth-century society is embodied in the changing fortunes of the two principal types of Italian opera – *opera seria* and *opera buffa*. The difference between these is much more than just the difference between 'serious' and 'comic'. Where the first was concerned with stories of gods and heroic figures drawn from antiquity, the second was concerned with ordinary characters (often servants) drawn from contemporary life. Where *opera seria* cultivated a high tone of baroque tragedy, *opera buffa* favoured a much more direct, down-to-earth tone and delivery. Its democratic aspect was thus derived not only from its subject matter but also from its style. Though Naples was a key centre and most of its key composers were Italian (Pergolesi, Galuppi, Piccinni, Cimarosa, Paisiello), the form was hugely popular and spread quickly across Europe.

The basic plot of all *opera buffe* was precisely the social tensions (and attendant comedy) between the aristocratic and everyday, the high and low, the serious and the comic, the ideal and the mundane. At its heart was a reversal of the usual social hierarchies in which servants get the better of their masters and women often get the better of the men. What might be socially and politically disturbing in a more serious setting, was perfectly acceptable as the plot of a comic opera. Musically, *opera buffa* was distinguished from its more serious counterpart by a simpler and more direct musical style: where *opera seria* had baroque da capo arias and highly decorated cantilena lines, *opera buffa* had simple strophic songs in short phrases and plain rhythms. This opposition was itself exploited in *opera buffa*, to mark out a character either as of noble birth or as having pretensions to nobility – either way, the style lent itself easily to parody. Part of the popularity of *opera buffa* lay in its much faster pace and rapid changes of direction whereas *opera seria* tended to be more static and contemplative. It depended on the familiarity of its conventions since the eighteenth-century audience did not sit in quiet concentration as is the habit today. Conventions included stock character types and situations (the innocent young girl of lower social status desired by the older, rather ridiculous old man of higher status, or the scheming servant who outwits his or her master) as well as musical devices by which the story is told (the sequence of arias and recitatives, but also musical 'styles' and voices associated with different character types, such as a rustic simplicity for the servants, or a tendency to pompous repetition for the old fool). Such conventions conferred a directness and clarity to what were often complex plots, but they also provided an endless source of humour – as conventions were subverted and mixed up to imply different things about the character or situation being represented. The very familiarity of stock characters and musical devices was part of the pleasure, an aspect of *opera buffa* taken directly into classical instrumental music.

Mozart's *Le nozze di Figaro* (1786) is a relatively late example of the *opera buffa* genre and considerably more sophisticated than examples from earlier in the century. It remains one of the most perennially popular operas of all time. In its own day, it risked censorship for the political nature of its plot, based on one of three plays by Pierre-Augustin Caron de Beaumarchais. *La folle journée ou Le mariage du Figaro* was immortalized by Mozart's opera whereas *Le barbier de Séville ou La précaution inutile* was later to be the basis of *Il barbiere de Siviglia* by Rossini. Though a comedy about class and sex, in the troubled political years leading up to the French Revolution, Beaumarchais' plays had been banned in Austria by the Emperor. Set as an opera, it seems, it was deemed to be less offensive, but it is not hard to see why it would have had wide appeal. Mozart's Vienna was already showing signs of social change as the privilege of an old aristocracy was increasingly challenged by a vigorous mercantile and socially dynamic middle class. Mozart's operas reflected something of this fast-changing world, in which appearance was everything and characters changed status according to their manner of speech and dress. The device of disguise by which characters changed identity was generally a comic one, but is often used in Mozart to more poignant ends – as a means of experimenting with different identities and trying out different personas. Opera's fantastical world, related to the real but thoroughly fictional at the same time, must have seemed like a privileged site for this new sense of identity.

Keyboard music

While opera provided a vehicle for expressing different identities on a very public stage, classical music also explored far more private and intimate kinds of music making. One of the most important developments of the eighteenth century was the change to instrument design that eventually produced the forerunner of the modern piano. It provides a good example of how a new instrument and a new kind of music go hand-in-hand. Baroque keyboard music was generally played on the harpsichord (or the *clavecin*, in France), an instrument not designed for making the kinds of nuance in dynamics and tone that we take for granted on the modern piano. Where the keyboard pieces of Johann Sebastian Bach would have been performed on the harpsichord, the music of his son Carl Philipp Emanuel Bach was written for the clavichord. A generation later, Beethoven wrote exclusively for the new fortepiano. Haydn, whose composing career overlaps with them both, wrote keyboard works that might be played on any available instrument, only stipulating the new fortepiano in his last works in the genre.

The development of the keyboard brought together two ambitions that embody contradictory aspects of the Enlightenment age. On the one hand, the keyboard is the triumph of the rational ordering of sound, embodied in the equivalence of the keys themselves, the regularity of their weight and action, their tone and tuning; on the other hand, the keyboard became the prime musical vehicle for the expression of the rich and subtle range of emotions explored in the music of the later eighteenth century. This became possible only with the gradual development of a touch-sensitive keyboard – first with the clavichord, and then with the fortepiano. Unlike the organ or harpsichord, *how* you strike the key on these new instruments shapes the resulting sound.

The historical importance of classical keyboard music is summed up in this one massive change. The emotion of the performer could be directly signalled through varieties of touch, translated immediately into varieties of tone colour and articulation. Composers and performers devoted themselves to making the machine more human – to make it speak and sing like the human voice. Mozart and his contemporary Muzio Clementi were once persuaded to take part in a famous competition to see who was the finest keyboard player. Clementi generously admired Mozart for the lyrical expressiveness and flexibility of his playing, achieved through control of tempo (rubato), phrasing, dynamics and tone. For his part, Mozart accused Clementi of quite the opposite – the cardinal sin of sounding *too mechanical*. Enthusiasm for the speech-like possibilities of the fortepiano led to the demise of the harpsichord, and few instruments were produced after 1800.

The clavichord was cheap, light, portable and quiet – a perfect instrument for private music making in the home. Described by the writer C. F. D. Schubart, in 1785, as a 'lonely, melancholy, unspeakably sweet instrument' it was, above all, an instrument to play in private. As such, it lay behind something of a craze in the 1760s and 1770s for cultivating a state of melancholy inwardness. Music for the clavichord provided a kind of aesthetic retreat from the outer world, a musical parallel to the cultivation of the private garden in the eighteenth century. The most important composer of such music was undoubtedly C. P. E. Bach, who wrote over 150 sonatas for the instrument, in addition to fantasias, rondos and fugues. It was in the freedom of the keyboard Fantasia that Bach gave most intense expression to the *Empfindsam* style – a movement within North German music in the second half of the century that cultivated intense and exaggerated emotions. The fantasias were deliberately capricious, jumping from one kind of emotion to another, apparently spontaneously, as if in an improvisation.

By 1800, however, both the harpsichord and clavichord were effectively displaced by the new fortepiano (later, pianoforte). Its popularity, in both the concert hall and the private home has never waned. This is reflected in the kind of music that was written for it: from Haydn's later sonatas and the works of Beethoven, the piano inspired a rich literature of highly virtuosic music, but also a wealth of relatively easy, tuneful pieces for amateur players. The keyboard music of both Domenico Scarlatti and Muzio Clementi remain in the repertoire today, wonderfully idiomatic and inventive music that deserves better than to be associated with the early years of piano lessons.

Haydn wrote around sixty keyboard sonatas over a forty-year period, with his earliest works designed for the harpsichord or clavichord, and his later ones most definitely written for the new fortepiano. Only the last of these would have been written for concert performance (in London), the rest would have been intended for domestic performance, mostly by women. The basic plan of his sonatas consists of a broad and expansive sonata-form movement, followed by a lyrical and often introspective adagio or andante. This was sometimes followed by a Menuet movement (which, alternatively, might replace the slow movement) before a vivacious and light-hearted finale. The sequence of movements satisfied the sensibility of the age – it articulated deep emotion, expressed the capacity for inventiveness and creativity, but also affirmed a collective ideal. Familiar conventions of musical form and style were sufficiently well known that both composers and performers had considerable scope for caprice in deviating from them in small but expressive ways. From the 1770s onwards, the sonata also provided opportunities for exploiting the possibilities of the new fortepiano – whether by foregrounding the subtle shadings of dynamics, the rich tone or the extended register of the instrument. By the time Haydn wrote his last sonatas, the so-called three 'English Sonatas' (nos 50–52) during his second visit to London (1794–95), his keyboard music was entirely shaped around the new instrument.

Mozart's twenty keyboard sonatas were written over a shorter time span than Haydn's and thus represent less of a stylistic shift. In fact, most of them were written in the decade 1774–84 and were clearly aimed at his own piano pupils and at the growing commercial market for sheet music. Whereas Mozart's piano concertos were written to be performed by himself at public concerts, the piano sonatas occupy a rather less important place in his output. Evidence that these were partly pedagogical pieces is clear in both the early C major sonata (K.309) of 1777 and the late C major sonata (K.545) of 1788. Mozart's style is so instantly recognizable that it virtually defines people's sense of what 'classical music' should sound like. The singing melody in the upper part, over a broken arpeggio accompaniment, interspersed with delicate passage work and a clear sectional form are hallmarks of his style. His music is also full of 'topics' – expressive devices that were understood by his audience to refer to certain extramusical ideas, like the pastoral, the military, or the 'learned'. One of the most famous examples is found in the 'alla turca' rondo finale of the Sonata in A, K.331, written in 1778. Here Mozart imitates the sound of the Turkish 'Jannissary' music (a kind of marching band) – a reference that had a particular frisson for the Viennese who lived for centuries with the threat of Turkish military invasion.

It is perhaps the singing quality that Mozart achieves in his piano music that is one of his most distinctive musical finger-prints. It is usually the upper voice that takes this role, like a soprano in an operatic aria, complete with ornamental turns, trills and runs. Indeed, it is the coming together of the vocal expressiveness of the melodic line and the delicate figurations only possible on the keyboard that really define Mozart's piano style and remained unequalled before the music of Chopin. Part of its expressive quality lies in the sense that it starts from the human voice, but then exceeds the capacity of the voice (in register, speed, tone). But this 'exquisite' aspect of Mozart, so-often found in his slow movements, is juxtaposed in his finales with a rumbustious and wilful sense of play and caprice. His rondo finales, like Haydn's, tend to set off without warning in wholly unexpected directions, full of brilliance, fun, and constant creativity that leaves the listener breathless.

The contrast between these sonatas of Haydn and Mozart and those of Beethoven is strongly marked. None of Beethoven's thirty-two piano sonatas were written primarily to please an audience or to be highly saleable works for the amateur pianist. It is significant that they are mostly dedicated to his aristocratic patrons whose wealth allowed him to compose 'at the limits' – pushing the boundaries of his own invention and imagination at the same time as pushing the limits of his formi-dable abilities as a pianist. When he arrived in Vienna from Bonn, in 1790, it was as a virtuoso pianist that he sought to make his mark. But his style was never that of the growing generation of musical entertainers, who sought to please their audience with displays of technical brilliance on popular tunes. From the start, Beethoven's attitude was that the piano sonata, no less than the orchestra, provided a musical theatre for serious and intense musical drama.

His first three sonatas, published in 1795 as his Opus 2, show little of the sense of play found in the music of Haydn, to whom they were dedicated. The first, in the stormy key of F minor, while outwardly using the simple textures of the Mozart style, has a kind of dramatic directness and single-mindedness that Mozart and Haydn usually avoided. The sonority of the piano is key to the success of this piece – both in the crashing scales and big chords of the first and last movements, and in the accompaniment of the slow movement where Beethoven achieves an almost orchestral fullness of sound. In their extreme moments of drama, Beethoven's sonatas seemed to draw on operatic models, complete with orchestral effects, but the next moment they can evoke the intimacy of the song or the pleasures of chamber music. This was already well evidenced by 1798, in Beethoven's *Pathétique* Sonata in C minor, Op.13. The slow introduction is not just operatic in style, it evokes the world of baroque opera. It foregrounds one of his recurrent and central themes – the attempt to make instrumental music communicative like the human voice.

None of this was possible without the resources of the new piano, though it is sometimes hard to imagine that Beethoven's demands could have been realized adequately on the instruments of his time. Almost all of his sonatas make significantly greater technical demands on the player than those of Haydn and Mozart, and hardly any of their movements could be said to reflect the ideals of pleasure and entertainment as understood in the eighteenth century. Instead, they epitomise a different aesthetic, in which instrumental music took on the weight and seriousness of literature and philosophy. Again and again, they stage a musical drama which was felt at the time, even if it was not understood as such, to be the inward drama of the individual, wonderfully symbolized by the solitary composer-performer at the piano. In his last sonatas, composed in the so-called 'late period' in the 1820s, the piano is often asked to exceed what might be expected of the instrument, in what becomes a kind of idealized music that seems to reach beyond the capacity of a single instrument and a single performer.

String quartet

The string quartet is by no means the only kind of chamber music that flourished in the classical period; you can find numerous examples of string trios, string quintets, piano quartets and quintets, wind quintets, mixed septets, string octets and wind octets. Nevertheless, the string quartet had a pre-eminent place in chamber music that it has retained to this day. One might well ask why this form, rather than any other, has acquired such prestige? The answer lies largely in the quality of the music that was written for it, but that leaves unexplained why composers were so drawn to it in the first place. Undoubtedly, the unique balance of the four parts (two violins, viola, cello) has much to do with it. The nature of classical harmony, based on the triad but often decorated by a fourth, dissonant note, meant that fewer than four parts struggled to give such a full sense of harmony and resulting sonority. More instruments would give a richer sound but also blur the transparency of texture that four parts confer (just as it had been for centuries in choral music).

The German romantic writer and thinker Johann Wolfgang von Goethe called the string quartet 'a conversation among four reasonable people.' This goes a long way to explaining why it appealed so much to the late eighteenth century and why it has remained such an important genre ever since. Music has meant many different things at different times in its history. At the heart of classical music is an idea that might seem strange to many people today – that music could be like a language, a kind of discourse, both expressive and thoughtful at the same time. Not *literally* a language, but *like* a language. It was not that composers thought music could narrate or describe literal events or things, but that it could proceed in a manner similar to language. It could present musical ideas (a theme or motif) and develop them as the piece went on – rethink them, rephrase them, consider them from different angles and see how they interact with other ideas.

If classical music as a whole came to be conceived like a language, the string quartet came to be seen as the medium in which this aspect could be most directly elaborated. The idea of discourse – of an exchange of musical ideas between four, increasingly equal instrumental voices – lies behind the classical string quartet. It was a perfect symbol of Enlightenment ideals – a community formed of equal individual parts, each having their say, each fully characterized, sensitive and subtle, each 'free', but nevertheless reaching agreement through exchange and rational discussion. It was a sign of a new status for music that was only just beginning to be voiced in the closing years of the century. In 1790, the philosopher Immanuel Kant could still suggest, in his *Critique of Judgement*, that music, 'since it plays merely with the sensations, has the lowest place among the fine arts'. Kant's view, that music could not be a serious, thinking art like litera-ture was already a conservative one by the 1790s. The rise of an autonomous instrumental music in the classical era (i.e. music for its own sake) anticipated a shift in attitude among writers and thinkers that would see, in early romanticism, a complete rever-sal of the old hierarchy of the arts.

It is perhaps in the string quartets of Haydn's mature style that one finds the best examples of classical music working like a language. The clarity of thematic presentation and develop-ment in sharply defined phrases and sections produces a sense of musical grammar or syntax. The balance and exchange between the four instruments creates a sense of comment, dispute and agreement. It has often been said that the quartets are a musician's music, that one needs to be part of the game to fully appreciate its subtle twists and turns. It is certainly true that, taken as a whole, Haydn's sixty-eight string quartets constitute an incredibly rich body of music – entirely accessible works, but at the same time wonderfully ingenious and refined in terms of their musical language.

Because the musical conventions of the classical style were so well established by the 1770s, composers were able to play a highly developed game with listeners' expectations. At the heart of Haydn's music, exemplified in the string quartets, is a wonderfully warm-hearted but refined sense of humour. It occurs in all sorts of ways, but essentially arises from setting up an expectation that the music will proceed in one direction, and then confounding it by doing something else. It is precisely because the classical style had developed such a clear sense of musical logic that it was possible to subvert it in playful (and sometimes dramatic) ways, without the whole thing becoming incoherent. Because conventions of phrase progression, cadential endings, stylistic voices, instrumentation and so forth were so well known, it made possible all kinds of humour through exaggeration or deliberately 'wrong' moves. But before you rush to Haydn's quartets for an evening of comedy, it should be said that none of this is perhaps as obvious today as it probably was to Haydn's own audience (and then, probably only to fellow musicians). Undoubtedly time dulls our receptiveness to the subtleties of this kind of linguistic play, but the more one listens and becomes immersed in the style the more the wit of these works begins to re-emerge.

Mozart acknowledged a huge debt to Haydn in dedicating a set of six quartets to the older composer, written between 1782 and 1785. These 'Haydn Quartets' use simple materials but subject them to highly subtle and refined treatment. This gap between material and treatment becomes more pronounced in his later works, as in his string quintets (two violins, two violas and cello), which contain some of his most astonishing music.

The C major quintet, K.515 (1787) is a good example. Its expansive first movement, at 386 bars longer than some symphonic movements, is built almost entirely on a simple C major arpeggio. Like Haydn, Mozart plays with conventional expectations as a foil to unexpected directions in the music. He uses the strong sense of implied direction in the classical style in order to set off unexpected turns and digressions.

The first movement of the Quintet in G minor, K.516 (1787) lasts over fifteen minutes in performance, a sign that chamber music was assuming a weight that was foreign to Haydn's early quartets of the 1760s. It is not a question simply of duration though, but rather the complexity of the musical form that produces longer works. The middle section of the sonata form (known as the Development section) increasingly explores musical ideas and tonal areas apparently very distant to the opening section, often taking on the character of a musical labyrinth whose outcome is far from certain. At the heart of the classical style, itself a product of Enlightenment rationalism, there is thus a key moment of irrationality and mystery. Classical chamber music was the perfect vehicle for expressing a unified voice, but also opened up its opposite – the fragmentation or splintering of the musical subject. In this, classical music already anticipated a key move of musical romanticism and modernity.

Beethoven's output of sixteen string quartets began, in 1800, with a set of six quartets, Op.18, dedicated to Count Lobkowitz, one of his most important patrons. These are already large public works – weighty, serious and complex – both to play and to listen to. A further half-set (of three) appeared in 1806 as Op. 59, known as the 'Rasomovsky' Quartets after the Russian aristocrat to whom they were dedicated. These are huge works of around forty minutes in duration, composed more like symphonies in which the separate movements have a strong sense of belonging together and leading one to the next. After these works, all Beethoven's remaining string quartets were published individually, too large to be considered as members of a set. Two works appeared in 1809 (his Op. 74 and Op. 95 quartets) after which Beethoven appeared to have abandoned the form until the astonishing collection of five late quartets written between 1824 and 1826, including a massive alternative finale to one of them, known as the *Grosse Fuge* (the 'Great Fugue').

These so-called 'late quartets' constitute one of the most extraordinary statements in the history of music. For many years these works were widely dismissed as disordered products of Beethoven's deafness; today they are revered as works of genius.

Symphony

What do we do when we go to a symphony concert? We make a considerable effort to get to a large public building and part with a significant sum of money in order to sit slightly too close to several hundred strangers in reverent silence. While the music lasts, we are not allowed to move, speak, eat or drink. We ritually greet the arrival of the orchestra, who downplay any individuality in the anonymity of their formal dress. The conductor is greeted as a star, as if he were the composer himself. For up to an hour at a time, the audience sits in silence until the music stops. During that time one might observe that people are apparently lost in the experience of listening, concentrating intently though displaying no obvious signs of approval or delight. One of the most striking aspects of this, compared with many other musical traditions, is that the experience of music in this setting seems utterly private. Though people have come together in a public space, the emotional journey of the music is completely private. Only at the end, with the eruption of the applause, does the audience express collectively what they have just experienced individually.

This collective sharing of private experience is of course part of any performance art, of theatre or film as much as the classical symphony concert, but classical music seems to embody the idea in special ways. The symphony, the most prestigious and public of the forms of classical music, developed as a vehicle for the public statement of private emotions. In romantic music the symphony composer was practically expected to project an emotional autobiography as a kind of narrative with which the audience were invited to identify. This breaks the surface most obviously with Berlioz's *Symphonie Fantastique* (1830) and runs through the century to Tchaikovsky and Mahler at its end, but it was in the classical era that this idea was worked out. It is not that classical composers wrote works as a kind of emotional autobiography, but rather that the genres of concerto and symphony were increasingly concerned with balancing out conflicting ideas of the public and private – on the one hand, the rich inner world of moods, emotions and ideas that defined the modern individual, on the other, a statement of grand, collective and affirmative public ideals.

The orchestral concert, rather like the opera, was a place where you could try to balance out that very modern tension of being a jumble of private feeling while at the same time being a citizen of an increasingly busy, demanding urban society. It was a place where you could try to reconcile the differences between your need to identify with a public persona with the sense that, privately, you might not quite fit that public identity. This is what happens in the concert hall and the opera house and why there is something collectively reassuring about experiencing intense private emotions together. But the symphonies that are performed in the concert halls are of course themselves part of this process; understanding how this works – how symphonies already mediate this idea of public and private – is perhaps a key to grasping the importance of the symphony's role in classical music more generally.

Completed in 1804, Beethoven's *Eroica* Symphony exemplifies the ideals of the symphony as inherited from the later works of Mozart and Haydn: a work that made grand and affirmative public statements, that seemed to express collective energy and optimism. Beethoven's symphonies do all of that but, crucially, not without a struggle. The default position of Beethoven's symphonies is not simply triumphal affirmation, but the idea of affirmation hard-won through extended struggle: the 'heroism' of the *Eroica* is not so much in the blaze of E flat major and the prominent use of the horns, but in the drawn out process of musical wrestling that has to be undergone to arrive there. For this reason, the story that Beethoven originally planned to dedicate the symphony to Napoleon is both helpful and unhelpful at the same time; helpful, because it draws attention to the collective spirit of revolutionary social optimism that, at one time, Napoleon seemed to represent; unhelpful, because it implies that the symphony might be about a single, actual person instead of a drama that each member of the audience can internalize as their own. After all, what do we care about Napoleon or the French Revolution when listening to Beethoven today?

The symphonic ideal was founded on the idea of integration. A symphony necessarily involves a variety of elements – not just in the contrast of its different movements, but also in the different materials found within each movement, marked by the opposition of different key areas. What was deemed so powerful about Beethoven's symphonies was not just that they integrated different materials, but that they managed to open up such apparently vast areas of musical argument and still work through to the affirmation of some grand unity. The idea that the four movements of the symphony are themselves connected is a natural outgrowth of these techniques. Each movement becomes a different aspect of the same idea – but also a link in the chain or chapter in the novel, with the finale increasingly taking on a new weight (rarely found in Haydn) of the kind of dramatic revisiting and resolution of the earlier tensions – like an operatic denouement.

In the Symphony, the classical era found a musical vehicle for the idea of the sublime, a central category in late eighteenth-century aesthetics. In the words of the theorist J. A. P. Schulz, writing in the 1770s, the symphony is like heroic poetry, 'it lifts and stirs the soul of the listener and requires the same spirit, the same sublime power of imagination'. The cultivation of the sublime had to do with the sense of being overwhelmed by something that was too great to be understood by the rational mind alone, and threw the subject back onto the imagination. Favourite examples were the enormity of mountain landscapes or the infinity of the night sky – phenomena too vast to be grasped by the senses alone. The symphony increasingly offered an experience of sublimity not just because its orchestral forces were comparatively vast, and works became longer, but also because the symphony was a musical canvas on which composers could paint grander and wilder scenes than were normally acceptable in domestic music-making. The thunder-storm that forms the fourth movement of Beethoven's 'Pastoral' Symphony (1808) provides a good example.

Beethoven's symphonies are a long way from the origins of the form in various baroque genres of the early eighteenth century, and a long way from the early symphonies of Haydn and his contemporaries in the 1760s when the virtues of enter-taining diversity were more important than the intense drama of Beethoven's key works. Various forerunners of the classical symphony have been suggested – the orchestral sinfonias of baroque choral works, the Italian opera overture, the 'ripieno concerto' – but the most important development in the eighteenth century was less a technical one to do with the number of movements or size of the orchestra than it was a shift in the status of orchestral music. Baroque sinfonias are ancillary, attached to larger vocal pieces by way of introduction, but classical symphonies take centre stage. Here, the drama of the opera is no longer simply accompanied by the orchestra – it is internalized by it.

The development of the orchestra went hand-in-hand with this process as composers sought more power and variety of colour. To the basic strings-only ensemble were added, from about 1730, two horns and/or two oboes. In works with a military theme these might be augmented by two trumpets and timpani. The oboes were sometimes substituted by two flutes and the bassoon, present as part of the continuo group, gradually achieved a level of independence. Clarinets were not widely used in the symphony until Mozart's works of the 1780s. The orchestra, like so much else in the classical era, was not a single, fixed and universal form, but something constantly adapted to suit local needs. Only in the last two decades of the eighteenth century did it achieve what we think of as some normative form (strings, timpani, two flutes, two oboes, two clarinets, two bassoons, two horns, two trumpets).

Concerts and audiences

Though the orchestra flourished at aristocratic courts and in the opera house, the symphony is nevertheless inseparable from the rise of the public concert and the subsequent building of concert halls designed for the performance of instrumental music.

In the eighteenth century, concerts generally consisted of mixed programmes of orchestral, solo, vocal and chamber pieces. Where possible, performances of symphonies formed the beginning and ending of such concerts and were necessarily grand and generally affirmative in style and gesture. (Only 8% of eighteenth-century symphonies are in minor keys.) Writing such works for public concerts was quite different to writing music for a private patron; in many ways it allowed less risk and experiment and forced the composer to ensure the work would be popular and comprehensible.

The variety of Haydn's 104 symphonies, written over a forty-year period (*c*.1758–95), reflects the very different circumstances of their composition and the different functions and audiences for which they were intended. The orchestra at the Esterháza palace comprised less than twenty players, but in the 1780s Haydn began fulfilling outside commissions that enabled him to write for larger orchestras performing in public concerts – such as the Paris Symphonies (nos 82–87), the 'Tost' Symphonies (nos 88, 89), and the London Symphonies (nos 93–104). In the case of the latter, Haydn's last twelve symphonies, he was writing for an orchestra of about forty players who performed to a paying audience at public concerts. Another 'modern' aspect of these English concerts, unknown to contemporary Vienna, was the presence of music critics who wrote up each event in the press.

Though some of his early works were in three movements, Haydn's symphonies crystallized the standard classical form of a four-movement work. In his later symphonies, a slow introduction to the opening allegro movement became a standard feature. It was a means of emphasizing the scale of the symphony in the 1790s, acting like a slow curtain up before the drama proper began. Often Haydn used it as a kind of mock dramatic event, as a slow introduction in a minor key turns into a rapid, major key version of itself. It often produces a light-hearted effect along the lines of 'Troubles? What troubles?!' – the opening of Symphony No. 101 is a good example. Finales are similarly breezy and often comic in style (as in the Finale of Symphony 100). Haydn is rarely 'heavy' and never so in his finales. This was an important part of the public nature of the symphony as seen in Haydn's London Symphonies. These works are characterized by a sense of pleasure and public festival, quite different to the introspective nature of many romantic symphonies in the following century. Part of this inheres in the brilliance of sound that Haydn achieves from his orchestra – a sound that implies big public spaces and a sense of collective energy.

Mozart's symphonies run from his earliest works in the genre, written at the age of eight in London, through *Sturm und Drang* works in the early 1770s, to his last symphony (the 'Jupiter') written in 1788. Unlike Haydn, who wrote many of his works for private performance, Mozart's symphonies were always aimed at a public audience. The 'Jupiter' symphony exemplifies this idea of the symphony as public and collective discourse. Symphonies placed at the start of public concerts necessarily needed to start with a loud 'call to order' rather than something too subtle, and Mozart's opening here is in the grand style of an operatic overture, a fanfare and march with a powerful use of tutti gesture and force. The overwhelming sense is of civic bustle, public business, dispensed with clarity and well-directed power. By contrast, the second idea of the movement is in a singing allegro style and the closing theme introduces a theme in *opera buffa* style (the opposite end of the social spectrum from the movement's opening).

Something similar happens in Mozart's piano concertos where, typically, he assembles a group of different materials like so many different operatic characters and lets them all loose in the same movement like an ensemble scene from an opera. The balancing act between public musical discourse and private feeling finds a particularly expressive form in the classical piano concerto. The piano, as we have seen, seemed to put a virtual orchestra at the fingertips of a single performer. It could be immensely powerful, but also extremely delicate; it was a showcase for technical virtuosity, but could also sing with the simplicity of the human voice. In the concerto, the piano as a symbol of modern individuality comes face to face with the orchestra as a symbol of modern collectivity. The result is not a head to head opposition, or only rarely so in classical works, but an array of different kinds of interaction, as first the soloist then the orchestra takes the lead.

This idea of exchange and mutual commentary is built into the form of the classical concerto, which balances an alternation of solo and tutti passages with those in which both are in dialogue. The idea of dialogue or interaction is made visible in the solo concerto. The soloist, often the composer himself in Mozart's time, sits at the keyboard at the front of the stage, a solitary individual at the heart of the orchestral crowd. The unfolding of the concerto thus enacts a series of negotiations and oppositions, moments of reconciliation and balance, in which the audience is drawn into an enactment of the changing relationships of the individual and the whole. In later concertos of the nineteenth and twentieth centuries the relationship of soloist to orchestra is often far more oppositional, but the classical version is characterized by exchange and co-operation. The resulting musical form is a series of episodes in which the elaboration of the soloist often takes the music in unexpected directions – sometimes to comic, sometimes to sublime effect. The concerto, rather like the *opera buffa* to which it is often indebted, suggests a play of multiple characters, in which the individual often changes identity through disguise and masquerade.

The danger of the way classical music is portrayed today (as much by its fans as by its detractors) is that it becomes something fusty, old-fashioned, rather formal and pompous. The sadness of this is that so often the music is quite the opposite of all these things – time and again, it displays a kind of wit and liveliness of mind, always playing with expectations and often parodying musical manners that have become too rigid. In the big public works – opera, symphony, concerto, Mass – as much as in smaller and more intimate forms – songs, solo keyboard music and chamber music – the classical style proposes an astonishingly rich ideal. Built upon a highly refined and sophisticated musical language and capable of highly subtle emotional expression, it is also frequently comic, full of energy, and irreverence. Cut through all the nonsense represented by plaster busts of the great composers and the dusty frock coats and wigs, and it is the perennial vivacity of classical music that remains its most striking feature.

Musical romanticism: 1800–1900

'The most romantic of all the arts'

In his rapturous review of Beethoven's Fifth Symphony published in 1810, the German romantic writer E. T. A. Hoffmann suggested that music was 'the most romantic of all the arts ... since its only subject matter is infinity'. The content of romantic music, he concluded, was 'inexpressible longing'. Yet only twenty years earlier, in his *Critique of Judgement*, the philosopher Immanuel Kant had dismissed music as the least valuable of all the arts because, like humour, it may be entertaining but 'when all is said and done, nothing is left for thought'. Writing in 1801, the philosopher A. W. Schlegel described music in far more serious terms, as 'an image of our restless, mutable, ever-changing life', and by 1819, in the first edition of his magnum opus, *The World as Will and Representation*, Arthur Schopenhauer insisted that 'the effect of music is so very much more powerful and penetrating than is that of other arts, for these others speak only of the shadow, but music of the essence.'

This change in how music was thought about, accomplished over a few decades around 1800, represents a seismic shift in the nature of classical music. It marks a profound transformation in composition itself, but also in how people heard music and what they expected from it. The legacy of classical music today – and indeed our idea of the value of art more generally – was shaped by the philosophy of romanticism. The nature of that change is succinctly expressed by the quip attributed to Felix Mendelssohn: 'it's not that music is too *imprecise* for words, but [rather] too *precise*'. Kant's view was essentially that of eighteenth-century rationalism, which expected to understand the world through language – through reason, concepts and logical deduction. The split opened up by romanticism has its origins in a loss of faith in the adequacy of language as a medium for understanding the world, particularly the inward world of subjective experience. Suddenly, compared with the inability of language to get beyond the surface of things, the expressive quality of music seemed to go to the heart of the matter.

This massive reversal of the status of music, from a pleasant diversion to the expression of metaphysical truths, took place in the work not only of philosophers but also writers and poets as well as composers. It signals a much broader shift from the Enlightenment optimism that the world was rational and could be understood as such, by detached observation and logical thought. While such an idea was not in doubt for nineteenth-century science and technology, the arts were far more concerned with the nature of individual experience – with the interiority and inwardness of subjective life. Here, the logic of words seemed increasingly clumsy next to the ineffable quality of music. So whereas the apparent 'vagueness' of musical meaning lowered its status in the eyes of eighteenth-century thinkers, it was precisely the reason for its elevation in the nineteenth century. Music, as Schopenhauer's words suggested, appeared to be a model for the inner life.

For writers like E. T. A. Hoffmann, the music of Mozart was already romantic since it opened up the realm of the supernatural (in *Don Giovanni*, for example) and called into question the truth of the everyday, outward world. But it was Beethoven that was to embody this idea, not only for his own generation but for the entire nineteenth century. Beethoven became a kind of model, both of what a composer should be and what music should do. Above all, Beethoven represented the idea of the solitary musical genius who stood outside of society, creating works that somehow transcended the usual limits of musical logic and form. No longer tied to ancillary functions at court or in the service of the church, Beethoven's music was seen as outlining a freedom that was that of the modern individual. His works were heard as the direct result of his own life, the product of his suffering and his triumphs, the spoils of wrestling with his own life and fate.

The myth of Beethoven was undoubtedly more significant for later generations than the historical realities of his life. Though it was rooted in some facts – the solitude that resulted from his deafness, his brusque manner, his dismissive attitude to those that struggled to understand his music – our image of Beethoven is no doubt as contrived as those portraits of him with a shock of wild hair and eyes gazing heavenwards. But behind the myth lies the music, and though the music is equally subject to being reshaped in its reception, it presents to us, as it did to his own generation, something sufficiently extraordinary that it cannot be dissolved away or dismissed merely as the result of historical myth and our own credulity.

Whether one believes or not in the idea of artworks inscribing the inward struggles of the artist himself, Beethoven's works construct a series of monumental musical struggles, shaped by a vocabulary of striving, overcoming, triumph, loss and regret – from his first over-energetic piano sonatas (1796), through the *Eroica* Symphony (1803), to the late quartets (1824–26). At the same time his music amplifies Haydn's sense of musical irony, playing with the conventions of his musical language in ways that suggest a thoroughly modern self-consciousness – the musical language is contingent (it might go differently) and with it, the identity carried by the music is contingent. Beethoven took every important form of his classical predecessors – the sonata, symphony, concerto, overture, string quartet, piano trio,

Mass, opera – and turned it into a vehicle for exploring the limits of human subjectivity. It was perhaps this pushing at the limits, constantly crossing boundaries of musical form and grammar, that both bewildered and beguiled his contemporaries.

For the nineteenth century, Beethoven embodied the idea of 'absolute music' – a music that required no words to give it meaning, nor any extraneous function to define its value. What Hoffmann located in Beethoven's music was something both articulate and untranslatable, profoundly expressive of the inner life and the nature of human experience, but not reducible to a verbal content. It was essentially this idea that shaped the development of instrumental classical music for the next two hundred years.

Music of the future

Beethoven is said to have remarked, after a new work had been received with incomprehension and bemusement, 'these works are not for you, but for a future generation'. We normally think of the idea of an avant-garde, a music self-consciously 'ahead of its time', as belonging to the twentieth century. Yet our idea of Beethoven is also partly founded on this idea. To any composer or audience before Beethoven, the idea of writing music in the full knowledge that the audience would struggle with it would have seemed ridiculous. The eighteenth-century view of music as pleasure, never betrayed by Mozart even in his most complex or troubled works, breaks down in Beethoven. It is not that his music fails to please, but that this demand takes second place to a concept of music as self-sufficient, autonomous, following its own path no matter what. This is inseparable from the rise of the composer as a self-possessed genius, as a prophet or visionary figure, a heroic individual exploring the outer limits of human experience. Beethoven is an emblematic composer precisely because he has been taken to embody this idea.

A number of composers after Beethoven adopted this stance, as visionary leaders who advanced the path of music ahead of an uncomprehending audience. The great composer was necessarily isolated, because the public was always a generation or two behind. This view of the social role of the 'great composer' lies behind the notion of the avant-garde – a military term that refers to the advance guard, scouting ahead of the main body of the army. It had a profound influence on music from Beethoven to the late twentieth century, not least because it was an idea at the heart of the work of Richard Wagner. It was Wagner who made the most self-conscious statement of this idea of future-orientation in the nineteenth century. His 1849 essay, *The Artwork of the Future*, taken together with other tracts written while in political exile in Zurich – *Art and Revolution* (1849) and *Opera and Drama* (1850–51) – proclaims not only the role of the artist in shaping the future of art, but also of society.

Wagner's writings mark the beginning of a cherished assumption of modern art and music, that what is progressive aesthetically is also progressive politically and socially. It is no coincidence that these were produced just after the 1848 revolutions that swept across Europe and in which Wagner was personally involved (hence his political exile in Zurich). Neither is it irrelevant that Wagner was highly influenced by key figures of political philosophy, such as Proudhon and Feuerbach. Franz Liszt was similarly influenced by the utopian ideas of Henri de Saint-Simon (a founder of Christian socialism). It was Wagner and Liszt that Franz Brendel had in mind when he coined the term, 'New German School' to denote the sense of a specifically modern music, one which grew out of the idea of 'a music of the future', much bandied about in the 1830s and 1840s in relation to Liszt, Berlioz and Wagner. These three composers became emblematic of the idea that a modern age required new forms of musical expression. Those new forms of musical expression were above all the dramatic symphony, the music drama and the symphonic poem.

The dramatic symphony was primarily associated with Berlioz and was signalled by his *Symphonie Fantastique* of 1830. Although outwardly its five-movement plan does not depart much further from symphonic form than Beethoven's *Pastoral* Symphony (1808), the bizarre and often grotesque nature of its 'programme' places it in a very different world. Ostensibly it relates to the story that Berlioz had printed in the score, a drug-induced nightmare stemming from a young artist's obsessive love. (Berlioz had himself fallen in love a few years earlier with the Irish actress, Harriet Smithson, who after many trials and tribulations, did eventually become his wife in 1833.) Successive movements imagine scenes at a ball, in the countryside, but always haunted by the image of the beloved (via a recurrent theme, or *idée fixe*). Convinced that he is rejected, the artist poisons himself with opium and dreams that he has murdered his beloved and is being marched to the scaffold to be hanged. After his death, he finds himself at a grotesque 'witches' sabbath' in which a distorted image of his beloved takes part while the orchestra parodies the 'Dies irae' plainchant.

Berlioz brings together many key elements of romanticism in this work – the fascination with a rather grotesque supernatural vision recalls some of the disturbing short stories of E. T. A. Hoffmann. (It is worth remembering that Mary Shelley's novel, *Frankenstein*, was published in 1818.) But it is also an autobiographical story, albeit one distorted by deliberate fantasy. Though Beethoven never wrote anything quite like the *Symphonie Fantastique*, it was in the reception of his symphonic works that Berlioz found encouragement for his own idea that the composer's task was to 'write out' his own experience in aesthetic form. As such, the *Symphonie Fantastique* had a sequel, written the following year, *Lélio, or the Return to Life*, an astonishing mixed-media work tracing the artist's recovery from his nightmare and return to life via his re-immersion in art.

Later dramatic symphonies, like *Roméo et Juliette* (1839), dissolve the boundaries between the genres of symphony, opera and dramatic cantata in unprecedented fashion. For Berlioz and for other romantics, the forms of music were not strict conventions to be adhered to and simply filled with new material, but rather should be shaped 'from within' by the poetic content of the music. In the classical era, a composer's material might push at the boundaries of musical forms but it would rarely challenge them in any serious way. Works like Beethoven's *Pastoral* Symphony, with its running together of the third, fourth and fifth movements in order to narrate the change of scene from the peasants' merrymaking, interrupted by the storm, to the hymn of thanksgiving, departed radically from this idea. They embodied the idea of a poetic content taking priority and determining the form. In the romantic era, received forms were certainly not abandoned (think of Brahms's symphonies or Chopin's mazurkas) but composers felt increasingly free to invent new ones when they considered it necessary – such as Liszt in his B minor Piano Sonata (1853), which runs several different movements into one massive, thirty-minute movement.

It was this idea of dramatic narrative that lay behind one of romanticism's most distinctive musical genres – the symphonic poem or tone poem. As we've seen, the idea of symphonic music expressing a poetic content was hardly new by the time Liszt came to write twelve symphonic poems between 1848 and 1858. All of these have poetic titles that refer to their origins – in plays, poems, paintings, or simply the contemplation of nature. *Ce qu'on entend sur la montagne* (What one hears on the mountain) and *Mazeppa* both relate to poems by Victor Hugo; *Les Preludes* relates to a poem by Lamartine; *Hamlet* relates to Shakespeare's play, and so on. Of course, everything hinges on the nature of this 'relates to'. How can orchestral music, without recourse to words or images, possibly represent people, places or events?

The belief that it could, in some way, is embodied in the idea of programme music, one exemplified in these symphonic poems of Liszt and later in the tone poems of Richard Strauss, such as *Don Juan* (1889), *Also sprach Zarathustra* (1896) and *Sinfonia Domestica* (1903). It was a form that appealed to many composers in the later nineteenth century and early twentieth, including Modest Mussorgsky (*Night on a Bare Mountain*), Bedřich Smetana (*Vltava*), Jean Sibelius (*The Swan of Tuonela*), Antonín Dvořák (*The Water Goblin*), Claude Debussy (*La Mer*), and George Gershwin (*An American in Paris*). It was often taken up by composers associated with musical nationalism (see below) as a way of referencing historical events in national history or of evoking a sense of the landscape of a particular country.

The musical means by which composers evoked a sense of place or depicted people and events were drawn from the techniques of musical representation developed for the musical theatre – above all opera – and are today readily recognizable to most people because they subsequently formed the basis of classic Hollywood film music. Recurrent themes or motifs stand in to represent key ideas or characters; the different musical contexts in which they appear relate to the situations in which they are involved. Such materials are not arbitrary of course, but draw on the highly refined ability of music to denote character – whether the sense of flowing water in Smetana's *Vltava* or the arrogant confidence of the hero of Strauss's *Don Juan*. Strauss was a master of altering his musical materials, by orchestration, harmony, tempo, in order to tell stories in music – a work like *Till Eulenspiegel* (1895) anticipates in many ways the kind of precise paralleling of musical gesture and visual image we are familiar with from cartoons (indeed, in film music, the technique is know as 'mickey-mousing').

The question of programme music was hotly debated in the nineteenth century. The critic Eduard Hanslick, in his influential book *On the Beautiful in Music* (1854), argued that music

should not be understood in terms of things extraneous to it
(such as the emotions or extra-musical ideas it might provoke)
but only in terms of its own, purely musical materials and ideas.
For others, inspired by Schopenhauer's philosophy that music
had a privileged relationship to the nature of our inner life,
music was inseparable from the expressive content it carried.
Composers found themselves polarized over the issue – in
Leipzig, Mendelssohn, Schumann and later Brahms were associated with a conservative position opposing the 'vulgar' program-
maticism of the 'Weimar' school (Liszt, Wagner, Raff). This
polarity, partly fuelled by music critics and theorists, continues
to be reproduced in history books as the binary opposition of
absolute music on the one hand, and programme music on the
other. In fact, there is far more overlap between the two than
such a picture suggests. Absolute music was predicated on the
idea that music was profoundly meaningful, so much so that its
highest significance was embodied in a wordless instrumental
music. Programme music, at least in Liszt's understanding of it,
was not defined by any simple equivalence of musical device and
material reference, but was a way of drawing attention to the
ineffable poetic content at the heart of an instrumental work.
After a while, the whole debate begins to sound rather like
arguments over religious imagery between Puritans and
Catholics in the seventeenth century.

The idea that music was inseparable from poetic or dramatic
content lies at the heart of the work of Richard Wagner,
arguably the most influential figure in the whole of musical
romanticism. His conception of music, indebted to his reading
of Beethoven's music, not only shook the artistic world of his
own time, but was to have a profound influence on all the arts
in the later nineteenth and early twentieth centuries. The writers
Charles Baudelaire, Stéphane Mallarmé, Paul Verlaine, Thomas
Mann and Marcel Proust were all profoundly affected by
Wagner's work, to say nothing of his impact on composers such

as Anton Bruckner, Gustav Mahler, Claude Debussy, Arnold Schoenberg and Anton Berg. To this day his work continues to divide both critics and audiences, so what is it about his work that shaped so much of what came after him and leads his devotees to regard his work with such reverence?

Outwardly, Wagner's achievement was to transform opera, from a form still divided into discrete and separate 'numbers' (arias, duets, choruses, separated by recitatives) as it had been since its beginning around 1600, into a continuous, unbroken whole shaped 'from within' by the nature of the drama. Among his many ideas was that of the *Gesamtkunstwerk* (the total work of art), by which he aimed at a combination of the visual, musical and dramatic arts in which none would take precedence over the other. He preferred to refer to his own works as 'music dramas' rather than 'operas' in order to make this distinction, and not only wrote the words to all his own works, but was often involved in their design and staging. To ensure the optimum conditions for the production of his work, he supervised the building of his own opera house, the *Festspielhaus* at Bayreuth in southern Germany. His ability to do so, and to compose with absolute freedom (while living in great luxury) was the result of the support he received from King Ludwig II of Bavaria, after the eighteen-year-old devotee became monarch in 1864.

As the Florentine Camerata had done in the 1590s, Wagner referred back to an idea of Greek drama in order to propose something utterly modern. His early works show some obvious debts to the fairy-tale and supernatural themes of German romantic operas of Carl Maria von Weber, such as *Der Freischütz*, and Heinrich Marschner, such as *Hans Heiling*. The latter opera, for example, was a key influence on Wagner's *Der fliegende Holländer* (1841), his last work to still show some traces of the old number-opera divisions. Wagner's plots were often based on medieval stories and characters (*Lohengrin*, *Tannhäuser*, *Die Meistersinger von Nurnberg*, *Tristan und Isolde*, *Parsifal*); his monumental four-part work *Der Ring des Nibelungen* (1848–74), performed over four separate evenings, is based on Norse legend. But all of his works have an essentially mythic dimension, being far more concerned with timeless issues of love, death, power, fate and redemption than with real historical figures. The Ring cycle moves between the world of the gods, of men and of the underworld.

Wagner's concern with the mythic dimension of human drama was also a concern with psychology, with the unconscious, with desire and human will. Friedrich Nietzsche, a close friend and ally, wrote his key text *The Birth of Tragedy* (1871) around the figure of Wagner, arguing that Wagner fulfilled in the modern age what Greek tragedy had earlier accomplished; that under the form of real characters and events witnessed on stage (which he referred to as Apollonian), the music articulated a powerful unconscious content (which he called the Dionysian). It is perhaps this aspect of Wagner's music that accounts for his historical importance far beyond the opera house. Wagner took the basic premise of romanticism, that art's content and power operated beneath the level of everyday meaning and signification, and amplified it massively. Audiences were stunned by the all-consuming power of his music: some were thrilled by the experience, others were shocked.

Critics often located this power in what they saw as a 'cult of force' in Wagner's orchestration. His hallmark use of an extended brass section was seen as key to the 'new German school' and continued into the works of Bruckner, Strauss and Mahler. Others were dismissive of Wagner's leitmotiv technique, by which characters or key ideas are associated with recurrent musical figures. (Debussy later referred to them as 'calling cards'.) Wagner's radical use of chromatic harmony, often over extended periods of time, was frequently seen as undermining the basis of musical coherence. (The Prelude to *Tristan und Isolde* is usually cited as an example.) The extent of his musical achievements are perhaps evidenced, however, by the degree to which they shaped music after him, both in terms of specific technique and in terms of late romanticism's concern with a profoundly psychological dimension in music. Wagner's central theme, of an intensely subjective yearning for a redemption from subjectivity, lies at the heart of the music of Mahler and Schoenberg, as much as that of the painting of Gustav Klimt or Wassily Kandinsky. Even those who sought to distance themselves from Wagner, like Debussy and Stravinsky, were necessarily shaped by his work even in the act of rejecting it.

The sense of the past

What binds romanticism to modernism, and thus the nineteenth to the twentieth century, is that both are powerfully oriented towards the future while, at the same time, unable to let go of the past. The music of this age is self-conscious about its own modernity and therefore its difference to the past, but at the same time constantly returning to older music, sometimes in a spirit of homage, at other times more out of anxiety. Alongside the avant-garde tendencies of the nineteenth century expressed in the 'music of the future', runs a parallel concern with the musical past. Few composers escaped the foreboding presence of Beethoven – a kind of impossible father-figure demanding to be equalled or overcome. Schumann and Brahms both set out to write piano sonatas, clearly with the model of Beethoven's before them, but quickly had to concede that their own talents and musical instincts simply lay elsewhere. The figure of Bach was equally prominent – less threatening, perhaps, and more a symbol of the idea of a timeless quality of 'great' music (particularly, *German* music).

In this context, the 'rediscovery' and rehabilitation of Bach by Felix Mendelssohn is a highly significant event.

Mendelssohn's performance of Bach's *St Matthew Passion* in 1829 marks a historical attitude that, paradoxically, is a key component of the modern. Despite the fact that Haydn and Mozart had both paid homage to Bach's work in their own, his music had nevertheless fallen into relative obscurity before Mendelssohn's efforts. The cause was subsquently taken up by Schumann and Brahms, not only in important editorial work but also in terms of their own music. The presence of baroque elements in romantic music is curiously double-edged. On the one hand, it signals a kind of archaic manner; on the other, it was a way of by-passing the classical to reactivate what was seen as the irrational elements of the baroque.

This duality is often expressed in Mendelssohn's own music, which exhibits the same concern for formal order as his classical models (principally, Mozart), but at the same time adopts a romantic sensibility often shaped in relation to baroque elements. Consider Mendelssohn's Fugue in E minor – published as part of the Six Preludes and Fugues, Op. 35 in 1837, but written in 1827, when Mendelssohn was eighteen. Charles Rosen says of its opening that it 'may be the most superb pastiche of Bach ever produced with nineteenth-century means'. But the work uses Bach to quite different ends. It deploys a Bachian voice as a signifier of a certain kind of religiosity, but then builds to a virtuoso brilliance quite out of keeping with his model. As Rosen comments: 'Nothing further from the Baroque can be imagined in texture, form and general affective character'. Like Wagner's *Die Meistersinger*, written forty years later, this is a recollected past, a pastiche of baroque elements in order to conjure up the image of a world long past, and thus underlining its distance from that past even as it fondly, and perhaps nostalgically, recalls it.

Nor was Mendelssohn alone. Bach appears, transformed, in Chopin, whether as the model for his collection of preludes or in the fugal passages in his first piano sonata. Bach and Handel can often be heard as voices in the music of Brahms, even if only occasionally signalled, by the use of a chaconne in the finale of the Fourth Symphony (1885) or, more explicitly, in the *Variations and Fugue on a Theme by Handel* (1861).

Schumann's taste for the baroque comes out in many ways, not least for the *commedia dell' arte* figures that inhabit his collection of character pieces in *Carnaval*, Op. 9 (1835). His *Intermezzi*, Op. 4, is also a collection of character pieces clearly of baroque origin. The first, for example, begins with a grand, rather sombre piece of quasi-canonic baroque counterpoint, complete with double-dotted rhythms. But its studied historicism is answered by an unequivocally modern passage and, on a larger scale, the piece juxtaposes this 'baroque' first section with a whimsical 'Alternativo' section which replays the same basic musical material in modern dress. Schumann's *Kreisleriana* is saturated with deliberately baroque devices (appropriately perhaps, given Kapellmeister Kreisler's devotion to Bach): examples of baroque passage work abound, sequences of secondary sevenths, baroque ornamentation, double-dotted figures and bare contrapuntal lines. That these are baroque masks, not simply an innocent borrowing of musical techniques, is underlined by both the stylistic disjunction which arises from their placement and by their specific quality of exaggeration.

The monumental

At the heart of romanticism there is a strong urge towards art on a grand and monumental scale. Most obvious perhaps in the visual arts of painting and architecture, the same sensibility can nevertheless be heard in the music of the age. Beethoven's expansion of the genres of classical music, in terms of duration and 'weight', went hand-in-hand with the literal expansion of the piano (more notes, more volume) and the orchestra (more players, more parts). New buildings for music correspondingly reflected not just the demand for a bigger acoustic, but also the need to accommodate growing audiences. It is perhaps in opera that this cultivation of the monumental dimension was most apparent. In France, between about 1820 and 1850, the genre of 'Grand Opera' was distinguished from lighter, comic operas by its spectacular productions (including the obligatory ballet) and its large casts and orchestra. *La meuette de Portici* (1828), by Daniel Auber, is set in Naples and concludes with the heroine leaping into an eruption of Mount Vesuvius, an early example of the kind of spectacle that the audience now expected to witness on the French opera stage. It is perhaps the name of Giacomo Meyerbeer that is most frequently associated with French grand opera. Works like *Robert le diable* (1831) and *Les Huguenots* (1836) provided the kind of sensational and melodramatic plots and lavish staging that defined the genre.

After about 1850, though the tradition of French Grand opera continued, in the work of composers such as Jules Massenet, Camille Saint-Saëns and Charles Gounod, the profound influence of both Richard Wagner and Giuseppe Verdi was such that it began to lose its distinctive identity. In Russia, this was far less of a problem, in part because of its relative geographical isolation, in part because of a strong sense of national identity. A recognizably Russian opera was only properly established in the middle of the nineteenth century with *A life for the Tsar* (1836) and *Ruslan and Ludmila* (1842) by Mikhail Glinka. The nationalist sentiments of the group of five composers known ever since as 'The Mighty Handful' (Borodin, Balakirev, Cui, Mussorgsky, Rimsky-Korsakov), and the works of Tchaikovsky, ensured that Russian opera retained its own identity well into the early twentieth century.

The story of Italian opera in the nineteenth century is more complex, partly because Italian music was defined so exclusively in terms of opera, and partly because that definition rested on a tradition that went back more than two centuries. Where German romantic opera was fantastical, supernatural and philosophical, Italian opera was always concerned with the human. It achieved this, no matter what the subject or the characters, through the absolute status it conferred upon the singing voice. Where German opera was experimental, Italian opera was conventional; where German opera was theoretical, Italian was practical; where German was orchestral and symphonic, Italian was vocal.

In the early part of the century the conventions behind its success were established in the thirty-nine operas of Gioacchino Rossini. His first works to achieve lasting success, *Tancredi* and *L'italiana in Algeri* date from 1813. His most famous, *Il barbiere di Siviglia* (1816) was apparently written in two weeks. From these early works, conceived for the Italian stage, through to operas written in Paris in the 1820s for a quite different audience, Rossini established a set of generic and stylistic principles which laid the foundations for nineteenth-century Italian opera, remaining essentially the same for Vincenzo Bellini, Gaetano Donizetti and the young Verdi. Rossini's achievement, in addition to the astonishing colour and energy of his orchestral writing and his melodic invention and dramatic timing, was to find a way of balancing the static, contemplative aspects of operatic arias with the need for dynamic dramatic action. The alternations of these two elements in each scene he wrote are both clear enough for the audience to follow without further reflection, and sufficiently varied in their treatment for the formula not to pall.

The 'code Rossini' ensured the success of Italian opera: familiarity was part of a generic contract between composer and audience that was absolute. In unskilled hands it led to banality and predictability, but at its best it enabled direct communication to a broad public, without which Italian opera simply would not have survived. As Verdi once put it, in opera one had to compose 'with one eye on the music and the other on the audience'. But in a context in which music (especially German music) was seen as an elevated, almost spiritual activity, Rossini also became symbolic of the bad conscience of art. He achieved huge success as a composer, apparently without effort, became extremely wealthy, ate too much, wrote disarmingly popular and memorable tunes, and rather than progress into the tortured 'late style' of the post-Beethovenian genius, he retired at the age of thirty-seven and lived out the last forty years of his life in near silence. His hugely influential achievement as an opera composer was a product entirely of the second two decades of the century, which makes him a contemporary of Beethoven, Schubert and Weber. But his art was directed quite differently to theirs – shaped by the new audience and the new commercial situation of music. Looked at from this perspective, Rossini is a curiously modern composer in a world of romantics that were already becoming isolated from the broader public.

The same fundamental difference might be said to separate the way in which the music of Wagner and Verdi has often been dealt with. Wagner has been seen to epitomize the idea of the romantic idealist; Verdi, the idea of the modern realist and pragmatist. Verdi's music is hardly less 'artistic' than Wagner's (as if one could measure such a thing), but he was always aware of issues relating to the audience in a way that Wagner would have disdained. He agonized over the libretto to ensure that the drama was both swift and clear and never entirely abandoned the structural markers of the 'code Rossini', even in his late works. Those who find Wagner's music painfully long-winded may, of course, wish that he had taken a leaf out of Verdi's book.

It is in his music for the chorus, and the central role he gives to the chorus, that Verdi's sense of a popular monumentalism is most apparent. The presence of 'the people' on the operatic stage is key to the massive public following commanded by Verdi's operas and their real political significance during Verdi's own lifetime. The rousing chorus of Scottish soldiers that opens the last act of *Macbeth* (1847) for example, is out of all proportion to its role in the drama. 'Patria oppressa' is a hymn of the people for the people – a longing for freedom and an end to oppression. It mattered little to Verdi's audience that it was sung by a group of bedraggled Scots on a bleak moorland; such music was taken up by the Italian Risorgimento movement as their own.

It is an attitude that runs through Verdi's entire work, however, and one that distinguishes it absolutely from that of Wagner. His concern with drawing human portraits, extended not only to the usual operatic heroes and heroines, but to penetrating explorations of tragic downfall and collapse, as in *Macbeth* (1847) or his penultimate opera, *Otello* (1887), on which he was working while already over seventy years of age. It is a mark of the breadth of the humanity in his work that, having completed *Otello* he wrote a further opera based on Shakespeare, *Falstaff*, (1893), premiered in his eightieth year, whose eponymous hero is one of the few great comic characters of nineteenth-century opera.

As we have seen, opera had its origins in the tension between the experimental drama of a private circle of aristocratic aesthetes, and the much bigger canvas of public, commercial opera. Even Monteverdi's output was divided between these types. By the nineteenth century, opera was exclusively a genre for large public spaces, but one in which the audience expected to see the representation of intensely private emotions. Something very similar takes place in orchestral music, in both the symphony and the concerto. Like the opera house, the concert hall became a grand stage on which composers were expected to play out private dramas. From Berlioz's *Symphonie Fantastique* to Tchaikovsky's *Pathétique*, the story of the Romantic symphony was often one of autobiographical materials shaped into public theatre. On the other hand, a tradition running from the late works of Haydn to the symphonies of

Brahms seems to put more emphasis on the formal aspect of symphonic composition. This tension can be said to define both the symphony and the concerto.

In the case of the concerto, this attempt to reconcile the tension between individual and collective is, as we saw in the case of the classical piano concerto, dramatised visually by the opposition of the soloist and orchestra. It is in the nature of the concerto to differentiate the solo part with material that is highly individual and often mercurial, but also to find ways to mediate between the soloist and the orchestral instruments. One of the dramatic high points of the dialogue of soloist and orchestra is of course the cadenza. In Mozart's hands, and more particularly in Beethoven's a few years later, this began to acquire the function that it still holds today as an opportunity not just for the musical elaboration of material in an apparently spontaneous extemporization, but for its technical elaboration in a display of virtuosity that is thrilling in a purely physical way. There is always an element of the circus about this; as the soloist runs through his or her tricks like the acrobat on the tightrope, our sense of being thrilled is sharpened by the awareness that at any moment they might 'fall off'.

The idea of virtuosic display, essential to the romantic concerto, took centre stage in the first few decades of the nineteenth century. Its most famous embodiment has to be the violinist Niccolò Paganini who not only carved out the model of the international star performer, but ensured that it was associated, in the popular imagination, with diabolical power. Paganini was always a one-off, and it was some while before the works he wrote for himself were taken up by violinists of a younger generation. The phenomenon of the piano virtuoso, however, was more widespread. Figures like Frederic Kalkbrenner or Sigismond Thalberg, though hardly household names today, were the celebrities of their age, combining formidable technical virtuosity with a repertoire that favoured brilliant variations on well-known operatic themes – in other words, popular material treated with all the thrill of the circus performer. Thalberg was seen as a rival to Franz Liszt, perhaps the most famous piano virtuoso of them all, but both Chopin and Liszt should be seen against this background, with one foot in the arena of art and its elevated aesthetic claims, and the other in a commercial market in which the public got what it craved – showmanship and spectacle.

The poet Heinrich Heine once referred to a phenomenon he called 'Lisztomania', a surprisingly modern-sounding term for the nineteenth century. Liszt pursued a superhuman tour schedule across Europe for many years, winning the adulation of audiences wherever he went. When Schumann heard him play he was amazed by the sheer brilliance, but also recoiled from what he saw as its vulgarity. Writing to his wife, Clara, he distanced himself from a style that, he said, 'had too much tinsel about it'. What Schumann meant can perhaps be heard in works like the Hungarian Rhapsodies or, one of Liszt's favourite concert endings, the *Grand Galop chromatique* of 1838. What frustrated and perplexed contemporaries like Schumann was that this kind of crowd-pleaser was written by the same composer who wrote deeply meditative works, such as some of the movements in the three volumes of his *Années de Pèlerinage*. But Liszt rewrote the book in terms of what a romantic composer should be.

Another genre in which virtuosity could be foregrounded was the piano study, or Étude – a focus on technique that has occupied composers from the nineteenth to the twentieth century, from Chopin and Liszt, to Debussy, Nancarrow and Ligeti. A musical form that was originally designed solely as a teaching aid for the performer, to work at a specific technical problem, became in the nineteenth century a privileged site for single-minded experimentation in which music was allowed to be self-sufficient, elaborating textures and sonorities without care for set forms or musical narrative, variation or development. Undoubtedly it formed a vehicle for the virtuosity of the composer-performer, and both Chopin and Liszt were obliged to tone down their first versions of many of their Études that seemed beyond the realms of the possible for most pianists.

Such mechanical perfection and brilliance is a component of the concerto rather than its sole purpose; indeed, audiences would soon tire of a concerto that did nothing else. Instead, the soloist moves between the poles that have always defined instrumental music – mechanical brilliance on the one hand, and the ability to sing like the human voice on the other. While concertos exist for every conceivable instrument, the vast majority of romantic works are for either the piano or the violin, not only the instruments with the most obviously virtuosic traditions, but representative of these two extremes.

The long shadow cast by Beethoven across the nineteenth century is nowhere more obvious than in the history of the symphony. As we have seen, the development of the symphonic poem in the middle of the century brought symphonic music into the realm of programme music, an area already explored in idiosyncratic fashion by Berlioz. Perhaps for that reason, symphonic composition fell off dramatically in the mid-century, only picking up again from the 1860s onwards. In the first half of the century, the composer who looked most obviously to classical models was Franz Schubert whose nine symphonies reflect firstly the practice of Mozart (nos 1–6 were written 1813–16) and, in the 'Great' C major, No. 9, that of Beethoven. For Mendelssohn, whose five symphonies were written between 1824 (aged fifteen) and 1842, the symphony was clearly a problematic genre. His models are both Mozart and Beethoven, but his music is constantly tugged between a respect for classical conventions of form, and a romantic sense of poetic content. No. 3 'The Scottish' and No. 4 'The Italian' are thoroughly romantic in their evocation of place but they do so more by their use of folk melodies rather than through tone painting, which elsewhere he was perfectly happy to use (in *The Hebrides Overture* or his incidental music to *A Midsummer Night's Dream*). In general, these symphonies remain wedded to a lightness of touch more often associated with the classical than the romantic symphony. Schumann also drew on romantic topics of place in his symphonies. No. 1 (1841) is subtitled 'The Spring Symphony' and No. 3 (1850), 'The Rhenish', including not only the evocation of a journey along the Rhine but quite specific locations, such as the interior of the great medieval cathedral of Cologne. The fourth, in D minor, was originally written in 1841 but revised ten years later, and constitutes a much more forward-looking work than his first two.

Brahms's cautious attitude to the symphony might sum up the situation in the second half of the century. He began sketching a first symphony as early as 1855 (at the age of twenty-two) but it was not until 1876, some twenty-one years later, that he brought the project to completion. When people referred to it as 'Beethoven's Tenth', pointing out the similarity between the main theme of its Finale, and that of the Finale of Beethoven's Ninth – a conscious act of homage on Brahms's part – he retorted angrily, 'Any ass can hear that!'. Brahms once described the effect of Beethoven's legacy as like having a giant stalking one's every move. His four symphonies all find a balance between the classical model of absolute music and the musical language of the later nineteenth century. Though they are all in four movements and scored for a modest, conventional orchestra, they are entirely unclassical in terms of their musical language. Oddly, something similar might be said about the nine symphonies of Anton Bruckner (1824–96) despite the fact that Bruckner's style was always seen as indebted to the music of Wagner and thus as somehow opposed to that of Brahms. It is true that Bruckner deploys a much larger orchestra than Brahms (particularly in his requirements of the brass section) but, by and large, his works retain the sense of a four-movement and non-programmatic work.

In this, the works of both Brahms and Bruckner contrast strongly with the six symphonies of Pytor Tchaikovksy and the nine of Gustav Mahler. These composers both inherited a model of the symphony inextricably tied up with the idea of self-expression but it was one which, by the end of the nineteenth century, had become increasingly problematic. In Tchaikovksy's case, the situation was complicated by a further tension, between the tendency of Russian music to divide into relatively self-contained melodic sections and the expectations of through-composition in the Austro-German symphony. Putting aside the myths surrounding Tchaikovsky's Sixth and final symphony, premiered shortly after his death, and discounting the comments Mahler made privately about the links between his music and his own life, neither composer advertised the idea that their symphonies told the story of their own lives or sufferings. But that is not quite the point. Both of them deployed a musical langauge which was understood to be that of dramatic narrative, emotional disclosure and intensely subjective feeling.

The symphony, not unlike the opera, anticipated the role that film was to later to play in the twentieth century: it projected 'big' emotional dramas in a collective space, to which the members of the audience responded and with which they identified, in intensely personal ways. The continuing popularity of the symphonies of Tchaikovsky and Mahler can perhaps be understood in this light; the lyrical and dramatic nature of the music seems to speak to the individual, but it does so in shared, very public ways.

The miniature

It is symptomatic of the contradictions at the heart of romanticism that alongside the cultivation of monumental, public forms like opera, symphony and concerto, this was also the age of highly crafted musical miniatures. The romantic subject found expression both in massive public statements, but also in far more intimate musical forms such as Lieder and collections of brief pieces for solo piano. On one level, these works might seem part of the culture of domestic music-making, hardly on a par with the music dramas of Wagner or the symphonies of Berlioz. Taken at face value, many of the Lieder sung in drawing rooms and the waltzes and variations played in nineteenth-century salons might suggest no more than a sophisticated entertainment culture – a way of decorating domestic space little different to the furniture and curtains amid which they were performed.

But closer attention reveals that the miniature was often the place for a particularly concentrated expression of the tensions of romantic culture. Schubert's Lieder, for example, far from being unproblematic expressions of Biedermeier contentment, often show themselves to be deeply riven with the divisions of the age. The protagonist in Schubert's songs, as in the lyric poetry in which he found his texts, is normally painfully alienated from his society (usually represented by rejection in love) and searching for solace in nature. Schubert and his poets twisted this idea further: only by a loss of the suffering self, by a complete immersion in nature, is peace to be found. By this model, individuality becomes intrinsically dissonant and painful; its only cure is a loss of the self by a return to nature.

Consider, for example, the plot implied by the two most famous of Schubert's song cycles, both to texts by the poet, Wilhelm Müller: *Die schöne Müllerin* and *Winterreise*. Both cycles are concerned with the lonely figure of the wanderer, the individual who turns his back on society because he fails to find home and happiness there. The poetic conceit for that is romantic love; both protagonists tell a story of love found and lost. Rejected by the world (at least, by their lovers) the protagonists seek solace in nature. These songs construct nature as the only place in which the alienated individual will find a sense of homecoming in relation to a hostile world. But this homecoming is nothing short of a total immersion in nature – in Freudian terms, a regression back to the body of the mother. In *Die schöne Müllerin*, the lovesick young miller lays down in the mill stream and drowns; in *Der Winterreise*, the lonely wanderer who can find no resting place, freezes to death in the snow.

Müller's style represents the ideal of a romantic poetry written as if it were folk poetry; he was a key figure in the movement towards a renewal of German cultural identity through a cultivation of the German past. Schubert's musical settings follow Müller in evoking the sense of a folksong style, with melodies based on simple triads, repetitive motifs, especially rhythmic ones, and simple strophic forms. What mark these out as modern art music, rather than genuine folk music, are the musical deviations from the folk voice. It's not the more modern aspects in themselves, but precisely the *difference* between, on the one hand, a collective folk voice in which the individual is not essentially separate from the collective, and on the other, the harmonic, melodic and dramatic twists that highlight the protagonist's distance from this ideal. In other words, Schubert's evocation of an older, simpler *past*, is part of the means by which he highlights *present* alienation.

The language of folksy contentment, of oneness with nature and society, thus becomes associated with a dream image and of distant and rather fragile memory; present reality, by contrast, is empty, barren and lonely. Out of context, the opening of 'Frühlingstraum' (*Winterreise*, No. 11), might suggest a sweet, perhaps rather sentimental song about spring; in the context of this cycle of wintry songs, it sounds like a dissonance. As the second verse makes clear, this is only a dream, one that makes all the more painful the present reality.

This disjunction at the heart of many Lieder, from Schubert to Brahms and Mahler, is found equally in romantic piano miniatures. In his radical works for solo piano of the 1830s, Schumann deploys similarly disruptive strategies. *Carnaval* is typical of works made up of a collection of miniatures that feel fragmentary because of the abrupt discontinuities between them. Schumann's favourite ploy is to create the equivalent of the masked ball in which identities are blurred, and plural voices continually displace each other. The opening sequence of pieces in *Papillons* (1831), for example, presents a series of tiny pieces disjunct with respect not only to key, but also to musical style, gesture, texture and tempo. That they are linked by common motivic concerns makes, for the listener, at best a rather tangential connection.

In *Carnaval*, Schumann makes explicit this idea of multiple identities. Each miniature has a title, but these mix real identities (Chopin, Clara Schumann, Paganini) with Schumann's own divided voices (Florestan and Eusebius) and the fantastical figures drawn from the *commedia dell' arte* (Pierrot, Harlequin, Coquette). If that's not enough, the piece is wrapped up with his fascination with a real person, Ernestine von Fricken, who appears in various forms in the piece and whose birthplace, a town called Asch, provides a key motif for the piece (via its letters turning into musical notes: A flat, C and B natural).

Nothing further from a Beethoven sonata could be imagined, though this piece was written less than a decade after Beethoven's death. In place of the idea of a single, self-generating identity, Schumann presents a quick succession of quite separate identities. Musical voices are by turn heartfelt and ironic, such that they all become theatrical characters played out on stage; Schumann's subtitle for the piece was 'scene mignonnes', dainty scenes, a series of portraits like those that might fit into a locket, or else the fleeting glimpses of characters at a carnival or a masked ball.

The music of Frédéric Chopin is often seen to exemplify the idea of romantic music as public documents expressing private interiority, a music that speaks of intimate emotions – Chopin's we might assume, the performer's, or our own. But his piano works not only mark a tension between public and private, collective and individual identity, they also explore how those categories are bound together and how they break apart. One of the contradictions of Chopin as an artist is that, for all the virtuosity of much of his music, he hated performing in public and increasingly shied away from it. After 1832 (at the age of twenty-two) his music was oriented entirely around the salon – a private, intimate, but also essentially aristocratic setting for an audience of connoisseurs quite different from the public arena in which his virtuosic contemporaries made their living as modern showmen.

Chopin's miniatures, in particular the conventional dance forms of mazurka, polonaise and waltz, are almost always cast in simple forms. But just like the relation between Schubert's songs and folksong, Chopin uses a familiar form precisely to highlight the growing gap between the individual's experience and sensibility and something shared and collective. All three forms take a musical style associated with communal activity (dancing) but treat this from the perspective of the individual – a solitary and distanced reflection on dances, rather than real dances, vehicles for private drama and introspection at the keyboard. A solitary waltz is of course unthinkable, yet in Chopin's piano waltzes that is often what we get. Good examples are the A minor waltz (Op. 34/1) or the C# minor waltz (Op. 64/2): these are brooding, inward looking pieces. The melodic line is often displaced to an inner part, the energy of the dance hardly takes off before it's dissipated in chromatic sequences; the whole piece becomes an inversion of the upward, outward energy of the waltz as a social dance.

This is particularly marked in the mazurkas that often contrast two styles in the same piece: an archaic, collective, Polish identity on the one hand, and something modern, individual and Parisian, on the other. The opposition is played out between diatonic dance topics with strong metrical accents, and a tendency towards chromatic collapse and a loss of metric and tonal stability. The folk-like drone basses and dance rhythms end up sounding like *reminiscences* of a folk culture. In Chopin's last mazurka, Op. 68/4, there is an ultimate dissolution of the signifiers of the dance style through chromaticism and weakening of the beat. Its brief moments of physical movement are ephemeral if not imaginary; rather than going anywhere, they simply turn back in on themselves. This is the music of a wistful desire, which comes to nothing. It might be objected that, after all, this mazurka was Chopin's last piece. By repute, it was written on his deathbed. But look at almost any of the mazurkas and you'll find music that starts out with a certain forward-looking energy, a defiant, Beethovenian-type heroism with a Polish accent, but which very quickly, and quite unlike Beethoven, is distracted by chromatic sidestep and collapses into short, fragmentary sections.

Post-1848: late romanticism

In 1848–49, a wave of political unrest swept through Europe resulting in a series of revolutions and other expressions of political tension that were brutally suppressed and which left tens of thousands of people dead. Though there was not one single cause behind such diverse events in so many different countries, these uprisings related to an underlying sense of social and economic inequality. Why is this relevant for a discussion of romantic music? Because the widespread failure of this movement to effect change, fundamentally altered the collective spirit of much of Europe in a way that profoundly affected music and the arts.

The case of Wagner illustrates this very clearly. Wagner was himself closely involved in the political unrest in Dresden, as a direct result of which he became an exile in Zurich from 1849. It was shortly after this that his thinking was profoundly influenced by a reading of Schopenhauer's *The World as Will and Representation,* a work that had met with little success when it was first published in 1819 but, suddenly, in the wake of the failure of the 1848–49 revolutions, was being read with renewed interest. Its central message, of a turning away from the outward conditions of life in favour of the inward, seemed to touch a collective nerve. Where politics had failed to change the world, art and music seemed to offer a way of reinventing it inwardly – or, at the very least, offering some consolation for the imperfections of the world.

The profound shift of orientation is marked audibly in Wagner's work. Beethoven's music still projected the ideal of heroic action, opposing tyranny and changing the world (witness his only opera, *Fidelio*). But in Wagner's mature music dramas, for all the continuing theme of heroism, the ideal itself has become old and tired. In the *Ring* cycle, the god Wotan cannot deliver the hero he needs to sort out the mess created by his own greed, and waits wearily for one thing only – 'The end'. In *Parsifal*, the priest Amfortas is literally sick because his own strength of purpose had faltered; the young Parsifal may persevere where Amfortas could not, but the end of the opera is curiously insular, as if the Knights of the Holy Grail can now finally shut out the rest of the world. Above all, in Tristan, the greatest hero of King Mark's court, Wagner presents a treacherous anti-hero – an overwhelming statement of the individual's turning away from the world, from duty and from society.

What *Tristan* proposes is an idea central to late romanticism and to modernism: that art's business is not with representing the outward surface of things or social facts, but with a radical interiority of the self, one which believes it is one and the same with the universal. It is a short step from Wagner's *Tristan* to the French *Wagnerisme* of the 1880s, to Symbolism, to the metaphysical concerns of Mallarmé, Schoenberg and Kandinsky. The technical directions that writers, composers and painters took, which we normally refer to as modernism after about 1890, derive quite directly from this idea, back through Wagner to Schopenhauer and the aesthetic philosophy of the romantics. In direct opposition to the rational and linguistic concerns of the eighteenth century, this new art would be concerned with the unconscious, the irrational, the metaphysical, the inward, the non-linguistic: it would be concerned not with representing the world as we encounter it in everyday life, but imagining it differently, reconfiguring the ways in which we might understand it and ourselves within it.

It has been suggested that the onset of modernism is marked by Baudelaire's *Fleurs du Mal* (1847), a collection of poems that captures this sense of an impossible tension between sickness and disillusion with the mundane world and a passionate, utopian vision of something different. There are many possible responses to the gap between ideal and reality after 1848 – retreat into historicism, immersion in the materialism of the everyday, negativity and boredom, but also the cultivation of visionary and utopian ideals, whether political, religious or aesthetic. The art and music of Europe after 1848 is caught up with all of this, and cannot really be understood without reference to it.

One of these responses found its form in a kind of cultural and artistic nationalism – an insistence on individual identity at the level of the nation in opposition to the authority of foreign domination, as was a political reality for those peoples subsumed within the Habsburg empire. Smetana's construction of a Czech musical style is a good example of how art could give powerful voice to a social and political movement – in this case for independence, eventually attained in 1918. From the 1860s onwards, Smetana's succession of operas and tone poems on overtly nationalist themes helped galvanize the political establishment. His musical debts to Wagner were overlooked in favour of his use of materials derived from Moravian and Bohemian folk sources. It was unimportant whether these sources were entirely accurate; what mattered, was that his music was taken up as a symbol for Czech national identity at a time when the Czech people were agitating for linguistic and political independence.

Opera was particularly powerful in this respect, whether it was the apparently innocuous comedy of *The Bartered Bride* (1866) or the far more politically incendiary retelling of Bohemian history in works like *Dalibor* (1868) or *Libuše* (1881). But the capacity of even orchestral music to stir national sentiments, in tone poems evoking national landscapes and events, or simply in their use of folksongs and materials lent an extra resonance to works like *Má Vlast*. Smetana's work was contemporary with the development of a powerful musical voice of Russian nationalism in the music of 'The Mighty Handful'. Both operas on national themes and tone poems (such as Borodin's *From the Steppes of Central Asia*, 1880) articulated a sense of national identity, underscored by the use of folk dances and folk songs – still much in evidence in Stravinsky's *Petruschka* (1911) and *The Rite of Spring* (1913). The latter works remind us that the use of archaic and popular materials, far from being a conservative element of music, was frequently employed as a kind of modernism, a way of breaking out of received musical languages, challenging the rather over-sophisticated vocabulary of European art music with the energy and particularity of asymmetric rhythms and modal melodies. It reminds us also, that by the end of the nineteenth century, the classical ideal of a universal musical language had been exposed as a historical myth.

6

Understanding modern music: after 1900

Throughout this book I've suggested that the changing nature of European music is bound up with the changing nature of European society, in terms of who made music, where, and for what purpose. As a feudal world dominated by church and court gave way to a modern, mercantile and urban society, the place of music changed and with it the kind of music people wanted. The growth of the opera house and concert hall, and the audiences that filled them, marked a very different kind of musical practice to that of Renaissance courts or medieval monasteries. But the outward changes in musical life, in terms of musical buildings, instruments, concerts, publishing or recording, have been matched by inward changes in musical style and language. Historical change is not confined to politics or the invention of new technologies; it also has to do with systems of belief, ideas, sensibility and experience. The changing expressive languages and forms of music, art and literature are both a kind of record of changing sensibilities and, at the same time, fictional experiments in ways of dealing with a changing world.

Nowhere is that more obvious than in the twentieth century. At times, the music of this period seems to reflect all too directly the century's bewildering pace of change, its conflicting voices, its mixture of irrational anxiety and over-rational logic, its force and its violence. But at other times, recent music seems to conjure some utterly different world – timeless and unchanging, luminous, delicate and visionary. It sometimes looks backwards – is nostalgic, even – but often scans the horizon of the future. All these elements are part of twentieth-century music, not only distinguishing one composer's music from another's, but are often present within the same piece. The diversity of this music, its heterogeneous and contradictory character, is that of the modern world itself.

Perhaps for that reason, twentieth-century music often seems to present a kind of barrier, even for people steeped in classical music. Many listeners feel far more at home with the music of earlier times than with the music of their own, to the extent that recent music seems the most alien to our experience. So whereas we wouldn't think of dressing in eighteenth-century clothes, talking in the language of the Elizabethans, or using the technology of the Victorians, we readily identify with the music of Mozart, Byrd or Tchaikovsky. We live utterly modern lives, made possible by the most recent technologies, but prefer the art and music produced when our great-grandparents were still children. This is an odd state of affairs and one worth thinking about.

Even the term 'modern music' seems to imply something negative. For many classical music listeners, the 'modern' is synonymous with music that lacks emotional engagement, is hard to follow, seems wilfully arbitrary and over-organized at the same time, takes perverse delight in dissonant harmony and aggressive gestures, lacks form and direction. In short, much modern music seems 'unmusical' in the same way that much modern painting seems to flout the usual achievements of technique and skill that one might expect from an artist. Worse still, for many listeners, modern composers seem to ignore what is taken to be a basic contract of art – to be expressive and communicative. Twentieth-century art and music easily dissolves into a host of '-isms' (symbolism, expressionism, atonalism, serialism, neoclassicism, postmodernism) lending evidence to the idea that composers and artists were preoccupied with their own sense of historical difference.

In this chapter I want to tackle that perception rather than brush over it and to think not just about *what* modern music is but also about *why* music in the modern age has taken the routes it has. There is a way of writing about modern music that implies a sense of necessity to the developments of musical language, a logic by which things like atonality or highly abstract methods of composition are simply inevitable. This way of writing has the unfortunate consequence of implying that the interest or significance of the music lies purely in its technical aspect. But there is a huge difference between the technical business of making music (composing and performing) and the aesthetic pleasure of listening to it. If modern music can be demanding and difficult (and some of it undoubtedly is), what is needed is not an account of how it is made in a technical sense, but an understanding of the experience and expressive need from which it arose. What matters about a piece of modern music – any music – is not how it was made but what it is. How does it speak? What does it speak about?

The geography of modern music

In Chapter 5, I considered how the development of musical nationalism reflected a fragmentation of the idea of a single musical culture, shaped by the movement towards political and cultural independence of countries formerly subsumed under foreign rule. The development of distinctive musical cultures in what was to become Czechoslovakia (Smetana, Dvořák, Janáček) and Hungary (Bartók, Kodály) are good examples of a growing resistance to the dominance of Austro-German musical culture. But this pattern was replicated across Europe and beyond, spreading out like a ripple effect as the nineteenth century gave way to the twentieth. At the heart of the reaction was a search for an independent and distinctive individual voice, a voice that was in part defined by its distance from an Austro-German one. This is what binds together the music of countries as different as Scandinavia (Sibelius, Nielsen), Spain (De Falla), Russia (Rimsky-Korsakov, Stravinsky), England (Vaughan Williams, Holst), North America (Ives, Copland) and France (Debussy, Satie, Ravel).

What is striking about this change is that areas previously considered peripheral (both geograpically and culturally) now challenged the authority of the assumed 'centres' of musical culture. The story of classical music, before the later nineteenth century, moves between a relatively small number of countries – Italy, France, Germany, the Netherlands, England – and often seems to centre on specific cities – Vienna, Paris, Milan, Berlin, London. But by 1900 musical culture had become far more diffuse; no longer confined to the same restricted circles of central European cities, musical centres were just as likely to be found in Moscow, St Petersburg, Copenhagen, Amsterdam, Madrid, New York, or Buenos Aires.

At the same time, the modern city itself became a theme for music in the modern age in a way that had been largely avoided before. Nineteenth-century literature often focused on the tensions of the rural and the urban – think of the novels of Charles Dickens, Émile Zola, Fyodor Dostoyevsky, Thomas Hardy – but there are few equivalents in nineteenth-century music. Only in opera perhaps, with the move to *verismo*, did the modern city begin to appear in music. Bizet's *Carmen* (1875) was considered shocking partly because its first act is set in a cigarette factory, and Puccini's *La Bohème* (1894), though often considered sentimental, draws upon accounts of the harsh realities of bohemian Paris in the 1850s. It was not until German opera of the 1920s (so-called *Zeitopern*) that music theatre directly confronted the issues of modern urban life. This appears in particularly arresting form in the collaborative work of Bertholt Brecht and Kurt Weill, whose approach is deliberately distanced from the subjective, individual emotion of romantic opera. Instead, drawing on aspects of popular music and avoiding the emotional tone of grand opera, Weill achieved a style that was both direct and peculiarly moving as a vehicle for the collective protest of an urban underclass in works like *Mahagonny* (1927) and *The Threepenny Opera* (1928).

If part of musical modernity was a more deliberate engagement with the modern city, another was its dreaming of being elsewhere. Music of the later nineteenth and early twentieth centuries is saturated with themes of travel and transport, understood literally as well as more figuratively. The song 'L'invitation au voyage', by the French composer Henri Duparc, sets a poem from Charles Baudelaire's collection, *Les fleurs du mal* (1857). Baudelaire's poems juxtapose images of the modern city, full of disgust and boredom, with imaginary, longed-for places in which the world would be as one hoped it would be. 'L'invitation au voyage' might stand as a metaphor for the flipside of modernity's love affair with the city and Duparc's setting of it reminds us that, just as real technologies of transport were changing the world, music was cultivated as a kind of interior transport – a transport of the soul.

Something similar is found in the imagined places in Tristan Klingsor's poems, set by Maurice Ravel in 1903, in his collection, *Schéhérazade*. The Asia that is invoked in the first of these songs consists of childhood picture book images of Persia, India and China. Its restlessness and desire for a different state of being, is symptomatic of Europe after 1848. One form of this 'turning away' from the everyday was manifest in the so-called 'decadent' movement of the 1890s, a flight into a personal world and a cultivation of highly sensuous art as a kind of alternative to reality. But the idea appears over and again, in many different guises, as a definitive tension of modernism – between the failure of social modernity to live up to its promise, and the longing of the human spirit for something, or somewhere, else. You can hear it in Debussy's 'transport' pieces, such as the aptly named *L'isle Joyeuse* (1904) and in the opening movement of Alexander Zemlinsky's *Lyric Symphony* (1923–25), which opens with the line: 'I am restless. I am athirst for faraway things'.

Time and space

The musical evocation of faraway places and the power of music to effect an imaginary journey runs in parallel to the development of real technologies of transport that were busy changing the modern world. At the start of the nineteenth century, the fastest mode of travel was dictated by the speed of a galloping horse, exactly as it had been for millennia. But, in the ensuing decades, the development of railways across Britain, Europe and America delivered a hitherto unknown experience of mechanical speed. In doing so, it began to shrink people's perception of space. A journey that took days or even weeks by horse-drawn carriage, was now shrunk to a matter of hours by railway. Vienna wasn't literally any closer to Paris but it *seemed* so, and thus, in people's perception, the world began to shrink. The rest, as they say, is history. The acceleration of everyday life, brought about by the railway, spread geographically and became accessible to a broader spectrum of the population. The development of the transatlantic liner, the wireless telegraph, the telephone, the radio, the car, the aeroplane and eventually space travel, combined to shrink spatial distance to a vanishing point. The telephone effectively negated space for a generation who perceived physical space in relation to the time it took to travel across; the telephone suggested that you really could be in two parts of the world at the same time.

The new experience of time and space brought about by such technologies was often the subject of modern art – the multiple perspectives from which an object could be viewed (cubism), the simultaneity of time (futurism) and its fragmentation and reversibility (surrealism). Directors of early film, in the first decades of the new century, discovered that they had complete control over the sequence and speed of temporal events. It is quite a shock to be reminded that Mahler's career overlapped with the early years of film or that Saint-Saëns was among those composers drawn to writing early film scores. A generation later, in the 1920s and 1930s, composers listened to music recorded on disc and had their music broadcast on the radio. The technology of sound recording changed everything in music – its audience, its function, its presentation, the very nature of what music is – but it is perhaps how recording changes the conception of musical time that affected composers most profoundly. Composers learnt what experimental film directors had learned, that the mechanical recording of events in time allowed one to manipulate it in new ways: the linear, organic passage of time could be, quite literally, cut up, fragmented, reversed and superimposed. Time was suddenly pliable in a way that it had not been before, an experience that was both exhilarating and bewildering, that drove people enthusiastically into the modern age at the same time that it made them nostalgic for the idea of a simpler existence.

Both experiences are part of the modern, as can be heard very clearly in Stravinsky's music. The block forms with which Stravinsky worked, parallel the experiments with time in avant-garde Russian film, and yet use material which evokes some ancient, pre-modern Russian folk culture. T. S. Eliot, hearing a performance of The *Rite of Spring* in the 1920s, heard not primeval rituals, but the disjointed noises of the modern city. In America, the lone figure of Charles Ives, knowing nothing of avant-garde Russian film or sound recording, was nevertheless captivated by the idea of the simultaneity of different kinds of music. The rather mystical effect of different kinds of temporal experience is captured in his *The Unanswered Question*; more obviously urban, if not riotous examples can be heard in *Central Park in the Dark*, or 'Putnam's Camp', the second movement of his *Three Places in New England*. The coming together of different musical groups, playing different tunes at different speeds and in different keys is one of the most trenchant musical symbols of the modern experience of a world which was plural, multi-layered and richly dissonant in its simultaneity of different elements.

It is perhaps this new sense of time that accounts for some of the most radical and often unsettling aspects of twentieth-century music. Whereas nineteenth-century music often works rather like literature, twentieth-century music is more like abstract painting or architecture, in which spatial and colouristic concerns take precedence over narrative ones. The idea of time in music is so taken for granted that we can easily miss the way in which it is reconfigured by different kinds of music. Our sense that the passage of time accelerates or slows in music is of course an illusion. Outwardly, a piece takes place in clock time: it lasts ten minutes or five; you can map it electronically against a rigid grid of subdivided seconds. But our responses to music are influenced very considerably by the different ways in which music *shapes* time and thus offers different *experiences* of time. A motet by Thomas Tallis constructs time in a different way to a sonata by Haydn, which is different again to a Webern orchestral piece or a work for six pianos by Steve Reich. Our experience of time is shaped differently by these works. In some, it's shaped by linear movement towards closure or structural climax; in others, it seems to change in intensity but without clear subdivisions. In some pieces change is predictable and gradual; in others, sudden and without apparent pattern.

Our 'commonsense' notion of how music goes is founded on the idea of tonal harmony that shaped music for three hundred years from *c*.1600 to *c*.1900. It is by no means insignificant that our 'commonsense' notion of representational painting is founded on the technique of perspective that shaped the visual arts for roughly the same period. By the early twentieth century, music was beginning to explore kinds of experience not easily accounted for within tonality, just as painting was beginning to look beyond a naturalistic use of perspective. This has often been construed in negative terms, in both music and painting, but might be better understood simply as art's response to a changing world. As ideas, beliefs and experience changed in the modern world, so art sought new ways to embody and explore new sensibilities.

Undoubtedly this sometimes involved negative emotions: the Expressionism of Schoenberg's music or Oskar Kokoschka's paintings in the decade before the First World War, suggests some of the violent anxiety of the age. But the flipside of this was the quest to find a language that could break through the materialism of the age and give voice to a more spiritual consciousness: for Kandinsky this meant leaving behind the representation of mere objects for an art of pure colour and form; for Schoenberg, it meant breaking through the post-Wagnerian chromatic language of erotic yearning to a state of completion – a new order. You can hear this quest in his Second String Quartet (1908); it finds its technical expression in his vast, unfinished oratorio *Die Jakobsleiter* (1922), in which the soul, at the moment of death, finds completion in the atonality of the closing section.

Music and technology

It was the Italian Futurists who first made artworks that foregrounded the link between the technology of the modern world and new modes of perception. They insisted that the role of modern art was to explore, intensify and celebrate this new experience. Soon after Filippo Marinetti published *The Manifesto of Futurist Poetry*, his fellow futurist Balilla Pratella published, in March 1911, his *Technical Manifesto of Futurist Music*. In this he urged that music should incorporate 'the musical soul of crowds, of great industrial plants, of trains, of transatlantic liners, of armoured warships, of automobiles, [and] of aeroplanes'. Two years later, the composer Luigi Russolo responded with his *Art of Noises* in which he made clear that the expansion of available sounds was to be found not in the conventional orchestra but only through the invention of quite new instruments, insisting that 'we must break out of this narrow circle of pure music sounds and conquer the infinite variety of noise sounds'. He set about demonstrating this by building new noise-making machines, which he called *Intonarumori*. Fifteen of these had been built as early as 1913, including the *scoppiatore* (the exploder) and the *ululatore* (the howler), which were demonstrated in a concert in Milan that ended in a riot (in the same year, 1913, that the first performance of Stravinsky's *Rite of Spring* caused a riot in Paris).

Though almost nothing of Russolo's music survives, he remained a key figure for later experimental and electronic composers in the second half of the century. Though he has often been seen as a peripheral eccentric, his call for new music to embrace modern life caught the tenor of the times. It was anticipated by a few years in the *Sketch for a New Aesthetic* by Feruccio Busoni, published in 1907, and even Claude Debussy, whose exploration of sonority never steps outside conventional instruments, remarked in 1913 that 'the century of the aeroplane deserves its own music'. A rash of pieces appeared soon after that self-consciously addressed themselves to ideas of speed and the machines of the modern age: Milhaud's *Machines agricoles* (1919), Honegger's *Pacific 231* (1923), Hindemith's *Music for mechanical instruments* (1927), or Prokofiev's ballet *Pas d'acier* (1927). One of the most extraordinary representatives of this movement was the American composer, George Antheil, who was working in Paris in the 1920s. Following his *Airplane sonata* of 1921, his big hit was the *Ballet mécanique*, premiered in 1926, scored for a huge ensemble of percussion instruments and including a host of non-standard instruments, such as electric buzzers and aeroplane propellers.

It was, however, the French composer Edgard Varèse who bridged the gap between a merely modish interest in the sounds of modern life and a thoroughly new approach to music. What is fascinating about Varèse's career is that it began by overlapping with a very French concern with instrumental colour and sonority, as found in Debussy and Ravel, but ends by merging with the post-1945 avant-garde and the development of electronic music in the work of Stockhausen and Xenakis. This journey is reflected in a literal one, as Varèse emigrated from Europe to the USA in 1916. His first major composition written there was *Amériques* (1918–21), a large orchestral work that captures his sense of discovery and new horizons.

Varèse was both a romantic visionary and someone fascinated by the science of sound. He preferred to refer to his work as 'organized sound' rather than as music, and set out to explore the nature of sound beyond the boundaries that normally demarcated 'musical' tones. He explored the 'cracks' between the notes of the keyboard by exploring quarter-tone tunings (i.e. half the size of the semitone), pushing at the upper and lower limits of instrumental registers, writing for massively extended percussion ensembles, and exploring new instruments – such as the *theremin* and the *ondes martenot*. For most of his life he was essentially a frustrated electronic composer, wanting to open up an unexplored universe of musical sounds beyond the conventional instruments of the orchestra. Only in his final years, from the early 1950s to his death in 1965, was he able to realize his vision by working with early tape players.

His exploration of percussion sounds, microtonal tunings and new instruments overlaps with the strongly independent tradition of American experimentalism that runs from Charles Ives, through Henry Cowell to John Cage and Harry Partch. But it was perhaps his desire to explore sound through the possibilities of electronics that has had the most lasting legacy. His own works involving electronic tape, *Déserts* (1954) and *Poème électronique* (1958), mark the beginnings of an area of musical composition peculiar to the modern age. Early electronic pieces, such as the *Gesang der Jünglinge* (1955–56) by Karlheinz Stockhausen, were painstakingly made by splicing pieces of magnetic tape, but it was the beginning of a technological revolution that is today embodied in computer technology readily available to any composer. While pure electronic music is more often associated perhaps with music that accompanies other things (such as a film), the manipulation of recorded and live sounds through computer technology in electro-acoustic music has become an important item in the toolbox of many contemporary composers. The dream of bringing art and science together is enshrined in IRCAM (*Institut de Recherche et Coordination Acoustique/Musique*), the centre in Paris funded by the French government and masterminded by the composer and conductor Pierre Boulez. Many contemporary composers have benefited from its resources – including Tristan Murail, Jonathan Harvey, Kaija Saariaho, Magnus Lindberg – but its achievements can aptly be heard in Boulez's own works, such as his *Répons*, for six soloists, chamber ensemble, electronic sounds, and live electronics (1981–84).

Music and popular culture

The tension between an 'art' music and different forms of popular music probably goes back to the distinction between sacred and secular music in the medieval era. And what we are immediately reminded of, by the music of that time, is that there was an easy exchange of materials between the two; Masses were composed on secular tunes, and sacred and secular pieces were frequently transformed one into the other by a simple change of texts. Throughout music history, popular dances and melodies have been taken up in a more formal kind of art music. If there is any distinction worth making between the two categories it often had more to do with who was playing, where, and for whom, rather than *what* was being played.

But when modernists like Stravinsky, Milhaud, Weill or Krenek reached out to music of the jazz age in the 1920s, they were doing something quite different to Haydn's evocation of rustic music in a minuet, or Mozart's incorporation of *opera buffa* elements into a piano concerto. By the early twentieth century, art music and popular music had become strongly polarized. For some European composers, uneasy with the insularity of what they saw as a tired European tradition, the opposition was marked geographically. America stood for all that was modern and progressive and a new energy – symbolized above all by the sound of jazz. There were few composers of the first half of the twentieth century, certainly in France and Germany, who were not touched in some way by the influence of jazz and, more generally, by the impact of popular musical culture. In Paris, the writer Jean Cocteau insisted, in his '*Le coq et l'Arlequin*' (1918), on a rejection of the prewar modernism, identified with Cezanne, Picasso and Debussy, in favour of something more immediate. Simplicity in art, he insisted, was not a form of regression but rather a refinement, and he appealed to modern artists and musicians to seek the purity of the everyday and the ordinary in the café concert, the music hall, the circus and in jazz.

For Cocteau, the new aesthetic was embodied in the music of his friend Erik Satie, with whom he collaborated on the

theatre piece *Parade* (1916). This 'ballet' is full of the wit, irony
and play that Cocteau later demanded in his manifesto. It was
presented in Paris in 1917 by Diaghilev and his *Ballet Russes*
company, with sets and costumes by Pablo Picasso and
choreography by Massine. Satie anticipated what was taken up
more generally by the group of French composers known as *Les
Six* in the 1920s and 30s, of whom the most obviously jazz-
influenced was Darius Milhaud. In Berlin, a distinctly Germanic
version of the same thing took place at exactly the same time, in
works like *The Threepenny Opera* (1927) by Weill and Brecht, or
Jonny spielt auf (1927) by Ernst Krenek. Krenek was originally
part of the Schoenberg circle, as an atonal composer working in
Vienna. But in 1924 he began to reflect on the nature of the
audience and the role of modern music. In 1925 he travelled to
Paris, met the composers of *Les Six*, and no doubt heard some
of the music of black American musicians like Josephine Baker
that was then seizing the imagination of the public and artists
alike.

The engagement with popular music was a central part of the
movement known as neoclassicism, whose other component
was a deliberate reference back to much older music, a stylistic
move that is sometimes denoted by the slogan 'Back to Bach!'.
Its main centres were Paris and Berlin, whose very different
cultures produced quite different versions of this movement.
Outwardly, neoclassicism seems like the opposite of a progressive modernism. Its look back to the forms and textures of
baroque music might suggest a restoration of an older style and
thus an attitude of denial or even opposition towards
modernism. But this is a paradox that goes to the heart of
modernism, a movement that was based not so much on a rejection of the past but rather on an acute awareness that the modern
age was irrevocably broken off from a past to which it was
nevertheless still tied. Neoclassicism, for all its wit and sense of
objective detachment, underlines that modernism is obsessed

with the idea of history and the past, but self-conscious about its own difference to that past.

Neoclassical composers thus never simply reproduced baroque or classical models in their own music, any more than they simply reproduced popular music. They took their materials from these sources but then treated them in ways that were unmistakably modern. The subtle deformations of these borrowed music models were often playful, but also curiously expressive. Stravinsky famously summed up the new aesthetic of objectivity with his comment that 'Music, on its own, can express absolutely nothing', and yet his own music is often heard as expressive. The act of distancing, embodied in the deliberate misalignments of lines and chords and instrumentation, becomes strangely poignant.

Stravinsky lived and worked in Paris in the 1920s and his ballet *Pulcinella* (1920), based on materials from an eighteenth-century *opera buffa*, is often seen as the first neoclassical work. The style is well demonstrated in his *Wind Octet* (1923): the motoric regularity of rhythm (rarely heard since the baroque) sets up a pattern against which the composer can subtly dislocate foregrounded instruments by displacing rhythm and metre. Something similar takes place in the harmony, where the expectation of a simple diatonic style is constantly skewed by unexpected turns. Unlike the sense of organic process in Austro-German music, neoclassicism tends to work in discrete blocks, sharply differentiated one from another, with the larger musical form arising from the permutation of a limited number of cells recurring in different order and combinations. Variants of this technique of subtle deformation can be heard in the music of many of Stravinsky's contemporaries – composers as different as Maurice Ravel, Francis Poulenc, Paul Hindemith and Sergei Prokofiev, whose *Classical Symphony* (1917) deliberately evoked the style of Haydn. Such works make a fascinating comparison with those of the Schoenberg School written at exactly the same time: both groups of composers were exercised about their relation to musical tradition and history but with very different results.

Principles of order

The significance of Arnold Schoenberg for twentieth-century music rests partly on his own works, partly on the influence of his teaching upon a wider circle of pupils, and partly on the reception of his compositional methods after his death. The idea of a 'Schoenberg School' acknowledges this influence upon composers first in Vienna and Berlin, and then in the USA after his emigration in 1933. A rather grander claim is made by the term 'Second Viennese School', which is generally used now to designate the music of Schoenberg himself and just two of his pupils, Anton Webern and Alban Berg. The label itself underlines that this movement was self-conscious about its historical position – the first Viennese School being retrospectively constructed as referring to Haydn, Mozart and Beethoven.

This group of composers is most often associated with the related ideas of atonality and serialism. The first denotes the absence of any sense of key, achieved by highly chromatic harmony and the avoidance of the usual (triadic) chords of tonal music. The second term denotes a way of thinking about musical pitch that Schoenberg developed in the early 1920s. Not simply atonal, serial music begins from the principle of ordering the twelve possible musical notes into a row (or 'series') which then forms the basic material of a composition. The row is something like a scale – a set of notes from which the piece is made – or a kind of basic melodic line from which everything else is derived. Schoenberg himself was often at pains to underline that, having invented a row for a piece, the composer still had to compose as before, with similar considerations of line, harmony, form and instrumentation.

Faced with such bald definitions, the perplexed listener may well feel none the wiser. Why would a composer take the rich chromatic musical language of Wagner into the realms of atonality? And why did a highly intuitive approach to composition in the 'free atonal' works of the decade or so before the First World War give way to the highly organized twelve-note system after 1923? Most accounts of the music of Schoenberg, Webern and Berg seem designed to put the listener off, and the 'method of composing with twelve-tones' represents for many people all that seems wrong with modern music – that it is abstract, academic, dry, unemotional, and far more concerned with its own 'systems' than with the beauty of the sound that results. I called this chapter 'understanding modern music', however, and I have no intention of simply reproducing a story that seems to me to mystify the music rather than make it more legible, so let's take a different approach.

A good place to start with Schoenberg and his pupils is where they started. Listen to their early works: Schoenberg's D major String Quartet (1897) sounds like Brahms or Dvořák. It is richly scored and full of lyrical melodies, and places him firmly in the late-romantic idiom just before the turn of the century. His *Verklärte Nacht* ('Transfigured Night') of 1899 is written for string sextet (two violins, two violas, two cellos), a medium notably favoured by Brahms. Schoenberg's massive *Gurrelieder* (composed initially in 1901–2 but finished in 1911) is his most Wagnerian composition, in terms of its musical language but also its scale. Scored for vast orchestra, choir and soloists, this dramatic cantata takes over an hour to perform and often evokes the style of a Wagnerian opera. The same late romanticism can be found in the early works of Webern and Berg. Webern's tone poem *Im Sommerwind* ('In the Summer Wind') of 1904 was really a student piece, but it shows the twenty-one-year-old as having absorbed the building blocks of Strauss and Wagner. Berg's *Seven Early Songs* (1905–8) are intensely lyrical miniatures, with one foot in the nineteenth century and the other in the twentieth.

Had these composers not changed style, we might still think of them in the same vein as Strauss, Mahler and Wagner, but between about 1904 and 1909 their musical language went through some rapid and profound changes, comparable to what took place simultaneously in the visual arts. In 1904, their music was still conceived in terms of a late-romantic tonality, in which a sense of key underpinned the music but was overlaid with an almost continuously shifting chromatic surface, creating a kind of intense and sensuous expressive quality. Within a mere five years, their music had moved into the realms of atonality, floating free from its tonal underpinning and shaped now only in terms of its shifting chromatic surface. It is not insignificant that Picasso's famous move towards cubism, usually identified with his painting *Les Demoiselles d'Avignon* (1908), was exactly contemporary with the piece often cited as marking Schoenberg's move to atonality, the Second String Quartet, Op. 10 (1908).

If such works were 'one-offs' they might have been dismissed, but they turned out to represent the moment when much larger historical processes broke through to the surface of art and music. Picasso's radical departure from the idea of 'realism' based on a sense of line, perspective and use of colour that was the major achievement of the Renaissance was certainly not confined to his own work. In the generation before him, Cézanne, Renoir, Monet, Matisse, Gauguin and Van Gogh, had all explored ways of using colour that undermined the idea of a simple naturalism. They did so for expressive reasons, in an age when art was understood to be valuable not simply for reproducing the appearance of the world (the new art of photography could do that) but offering intense and expressive 'viewpoints' on it. The German painter, Paul Klee, later summed it up in his line that 'the purpose of art is not to reproduce the visible but to make visible' – in other words, to make an outward representation of something inward, a feeling, an insight, a vision.

This shift in emphasis, from representation to expression, provides a useful analogy for what happened in music at the same time. In music, as we saw in the case of Monteverdi's madrigals, Chopin's piano music and Wagner's music dramas, a kind of sensuous intensity is achieved through making harmony more chromatic. The term derives from the Greek word *chroma*, meaning colour, so the analogy with painting is hardly accidental. Thinking about the magnitude of this movement in painting, music and the other arts, reminds us that such things are poorly understood simply in terms of the psychology or biography of the individual composer or artist. The shift to a different kind of harmony was certainly not confined to the music of Schoenberg and his pupils – variants of the same process can be seen in the music of Bartók, Stravinsky, Szymanowski, Scriabin, Ives, Hindemith and Milhaud. Most composers of this era were using a tonal language supersaturated with chromaticism, a style that persisted throughout the century in musical styles as different as the lush late-romanticism of Rachmaninov or the rich harmonic language of jazz.

To hear this shift take place 'before your ears', move on from those late-romantic early works of Schoenberg and his pupils to the works that they wrote between about 1907 and 1912. Good examples are Schoenberg's Second String Quartet, Op. 10, *Erwartung*, and his *Five Pieces for Orchestra*, Op. 16, Webern's Six Pieces for Orchestra, Op. 6, or Berg's Piano Sonata, Op. 1. Technically, what happens in these pieces is that the governing force of the tonal, harmonic framework is weakened to the point where it becomes redundant. The music no longer moves towards cadences and is no longer shaped by a sense of key, harmonic progression or clear linear movement. Instead, it tends to dwell far more on the moment, shaping a series of intense expressive gestures by means of a more freely dissonant harmony underlined by sudden rhythmic gestures and the colour provided through instrumentation.

In essence, this is not so different to what happened around 1600 in the Italian madrigal, when the continuity of polyphonic line in the more 'abstract' style of the sixteenth century was broken up by the modernity of the new expressive style, in which the sensuous intensity of each successive image suggested by the text was privileged over the abstract continuity of purely musical concerns. It's striking that what happens at the start of tonality (*c.*1600) is so close to what happens at its 'end' (*c.*1900). Once again, a hyper-expressive response to text setting played a central role. Just as the Italian madrigal was shaped by the intensity of a highly charged love poetry (achingly yearning and often erotic), so the move to atonality in the music of the Second Viennese School was shaped by the symbolist and expressionist poetry that often informed it – poetry that yearned for some transfiguring release from the everyday.

Text setting also provided a way of structuring music in the absence of the familiar building blocks of tonal grammar. Many of the works by these composers between about 1908 and 1914 were miniatures and/or song settings. Only gradually did larger forms return. The invention (or 'discovery') of the Twelve-tone Method, unveiled to his pupils by Schoenberg in 1923, has sometimes been seen as a way of overcoming this difficulty, but it is perhaps better understood as the product of a very different world. The early modernism of the *fin de siècle* was characterized by an intense subjectivity and a deliberate cultivation of irrational elements in art. After the catastrophic destruction of the Second World War a different mood prevailed. In Austria and Germany, the subjectivity of expressionism gave way to a new objectivity and sense of rational order. The 'Neue Sachlichkeit', of which twelve-note music was a part, might perhaps be seen as a kind of retreat from the over-heated intensity of the pre-war music, a flight into a more depersonalized musical language after the horrors of the war and the economic crash that followed it.

Schoenberg's insistence that using the twelve-tone method still required the composer to compose 'as before' is born out by the quite different results achieved by composers who took up the system. For Webern, the attraction had to do with a kind of geometrical purity that could be achieved when all the materials of a piece were closely related to each other. He was fascinated by different kinds of symmetry in music and often made use of canon (where one part exactly imitates another which it follows a few beats later) and palindrome (where a section literally reverses the one before it), both of which we encountered in chapter 3 associated with the music of Machaut. This often results in a music of cool detachment, as in his Symphony, Op. 21. For Berg, on the other hand, the adoption of the twelve-tone method was allied to a continuation of his own late-romantic sense of expression. He often arranged his tone-rows in such a way that they resulted in harmony that was reminiscent of a tonal musical language, a characteristic that often lies behind the powerfully evocative sense of loss in his music, as in his opera *Lulu*. After his death it was revealed that even his purely instrumental works are saturated with personal references and shaped by secret programmes. The *Lyric Suite* for String Quartet, for example, turned out to 'tell' the story of his affair with Hanna Fuchs, whose name appears entwined with Berg's own by means of musical ciphers made from their initials (HF and AB become, in the German way of naming musical notes, B natural and F, A and B flat).

The potential of the twelve-tone method, as a way of organizing musical material, was taken up by a highly influential group of avant-garde composers after 1945. The idea of the series of notes (numbered 1 to 12) began to be applied to other aspects of music – to rhythmic durations, degrees of loudness, types of articulation, and so on. The resulting idea of 'total serialism' (or 'integral serialism') is associated particularly with those composers who met at annual summer schools in the German town of Darmstadt in the 1950s and 1960s – Karlheinz Stockhausen, Pierre Boulez, Bruno Maderna, Luigi Nono, Luciano Berio, Henri Pousseur and many others. It was an extreme position, summed up famously in Boulez's uncompromising work for two pianos, *Structures I* of 1952, a piece that seemed entirely determined by 'the system'. In later years, Boulez talked about the sense of needing to begin afresh, of wiping the slate clean. In retrospect, this desire to step outside of cultural history, to start again, might be understood as a reaction to the horror of the Second World War, much of which only became fully apparent in the years after 1945. To a younger generation of composers and artists, the tradition they inherited often seemed to be fatally tainted, part of a catastrophic history from which they wished to distance themselves.

Unsurprisingly, total serialism was not a position that could be maintained for long, but the aesthetic stance of thinking about musical material and its organization in highly abstract terms defined the avant-garde through the 1960s. At the other extreme, was the chance music (or 'aleatoric' music) of the American composer John Cage, who had earlier been a pupil of Schoenberg in the USA and a participant in the Darmstadt summer schools. Influenced in part by his reading of Zen Buddhism, Cage developed a theory of musical composition that aimed to stand outside the ego of the individual composer. He achieved this by developing various chance mechanisms by which a piece might be determined – one famous extreme being his piece *4'33"*, a work in three 'movements', each of which requires the player (or players) to sit in silence. The 'work' is simply the ambient or accidental noises heard by the audience during the designated period of time. Though Cage's position seems to come from a completely different world to that of the highly technical and pseudo-mathematical rhetoric of the European avant-garde of the 1950s, the two produce remarkably similar results. Both attempt to distance themselves from what they saw as a discredited notion of expression and creativity and both produce results that, through the avoidance of audible systems of order, produce a music that strikes many listeners not just as inexpressive but as arbitrary.

The real history of avant-garde music in the second half of the twentieth century, however, is not what takes place at these extremes, so much as what was generated between them. The most interesting and significant music of the principal composers of this period is highly individual and difficult to categorize. Composers undoubtedly learned lessons and took ideas from the experiments of the 1950s, but developed their own voices and musical languages. Some composers have maintained an essentially uncompromising stance towards their musical language, such as Pierre Boulez, Karlheinz Stockhausen or Iannis Xenakis. But others have been more ready to change and respond to new influences, such that their later music often seems more approachable than their earlier music, such as Witold Lutosławski, Görgy Ligeti, Luciano Berio, Hans Werner Henze and Krzysztof Penderecki. Some composers, it seems, have simply managed to avoid being drawn into any particular school and pursued their own paths independently for the whole of their careers, such as Elliott Carter or Olivier Messiaen.

Such a list of names obscures huge differences in personal styles, but all these composers to a greater or lesser extent belong to the idea of a postwar avant-garde. Some of them have moved close to a return to older ideas of expression, while others have fiercely maintained the sense that composition is primarily an intellectual activity, a construction in sound. Throughout its history, music has alternated between these positions, trying to balance out these two definitive elements of composition. For many twentieth-century composers – Stravinsky, Varèse, Boulez – music is too vast to be reduced to something resembling the emotional outpourings of the composer, hungrily consumed by an over-emotional audience, little different to reading the artist's diaries or letters. In many ways, the avant-garde restored an aspect of music that was central to music theory in the medieval and Renaissance periods – that music was a kind of speculative thought, a sounding out of a world beyond the mundane. At its best, it springs not from an inhuman or unfeeling abstraction, but from the sense that the human spirit is characterized precisely by an ability to dream, to search and to reach beyond itself.

Colour in music

At the heart of Schoenberg's twelve-note method and subsequent developments of serial theory, there nevertheless lies a fascination with the abstraction of number. Schoenberg's system originates from thinking of musical pitch (the notes) as the most important element of music, and then thinking about them in highly abstract ways (detached from any particular rhythm or instrument or tone). This way of thinking about music is not new but it does become exaggerated in aspects of modern music. Perhaps because of that, in other areas of music its opposite becomes equally exaggerated. Running in parallel with the idea that music can be thought of in abstract, theoretical terms, is a musical practice that focuses on its immediate, physical quality as sound. If we think about modern music as starting with Debussy rather than Schoenberg, if we tell a French and Russian story rather than an Austro-German one, we end up with quite a different plot. Debussy's revolution in musical language is softer-edged and harder to analyse than Schoenberg's and, perhaps for that reason, has been less discussed by music historians and relatively uncontroversial with audiences. Nevertheless, it marks arguably one of the most important shifts in modern music.

Just as it would be hard to understand modernism in painting without grasping the central importance of colour, so too modern music makes little sense without attending to the huge importance attached to the tone quality of its sounds. This is not to say that colour was unimportant to painters before the twentieth century or that tone in music did not matter to earlier composers, but these elements assumed a different function around 1900. Since the Renaissance, colour had been subservient to line and perspective in an approach to art that was defined by the idea of naturalistic representation. Looking at a painting should be like looking at a real view or object laid out in front of the viewer. A painter deployed red here because the apple was red; blue there because the sky was blue. But painting was never photography; all painters have, to some degree, invented the world that they painted, not merely reproduced it. Any painter worth the name has played with the effects of colour as a creative act. In the late nineteenth century this aspect of painting grew in importance, as art shifted away from naturalism towards symbolism and expressionism. Colours were chosen not in order to reproduce external, visual 'reality', but for their expressive resonance, the way in which they helped evoke internal feeling rather than external things. Some painters remained figurative and representational even though their use of colour was non-naturalistic (such as Gauguin or Matisse) while others moved towards abstraction (such as Kandinsky or Mondrian).

A parallel case can be found in music. Sound is self-evidently a constituent of all music and no composer could possibly remain insensitive to its qualities, but like colour in painting, the quality of sound assumes a different role in the music of the twentieth century. Until the nineteenth century, composers often adopted a rather pragmatic attitude to exactly what instruments played their music. Bach's *Art of Fugue* can be played on any keyboard instrument since the composer seems to have regarded it as a compositional activity somewhat removed from actual performance. Mozart's piano concertos might sometimes have been played with one string player to each part, rather than a full orchestral complement of strings. Medieval vocal music may have been played with or without instruments doubling the vocal lines. But as the nineteenth century unfolded, composers became more and more particular about instrumentation. Berlioz wrote a *Treatise on Orchestration* (1849) that reflected his own highly original and careful approach to the tone quality (or timbre) of the orchestral combinations he used. In the orchestration of Wagner and Strauss, and the work of Russian composers like Mussorgsky and Rimsky-Korsakov, orchestral colour became a central aspect of the music.

A piano work by Debussy, say *Reflets dans l'eau* (1905) from his collection *Images,* is not obviously shaped by clear themes nor the kind of constant working away at a short motif you find in music from Haydn and Beethoven through to Brahms. Instead, the piece presents and elaborates different kinds of sonority, like different shades of colour in a painting. By using the great contrasts of which the modern piano is capable (soft and loud, high and low, dry spiky sounds as opposed to great washes of resonance), Debussy creates music in which sound, and the quality of sound, seems to take centre stage. Harmony and melody certainly don't disappear in his music, but they are not such an exclusive concern as in earlier music. Many of Debussy's pieces have titles that, in rather allusive ways, suggest some kind of visual imagery, often to do with water or light, and though his music can be highly dynamic and fast-moving, he often concentrates on evoking a sense of atmosphere. Elaborating space through colour seems more important in this music than elaborating time through narrative events.

When he wrote for the orchestra, Debussy's concern with instrumental colour and tone came into its own. His best known piece is probably *Prélude à l'après midi d'un faune* of 1894, a relatively early work that still shows plenty of late-romantic lyricism and rich doubling of lines in its orchestration. Even so, it already signals a quite different attitude to what one might call the 'syntax' of music. The haunting opening, for solo flute, suspended in time because of the elusive quality of the harmony and sonority here, has very often been cited as the starting point of modern music. By the time he wrote his tone poem *La Mer* (1903–5), his music had effectively become a kind of musical painting in the colours of instrumental timbre.

We often think of this aspect of music as peculiarly French. Debussy's concern with the sound quality of both the piano and orchestral instruments was paralled by that of his younger contemporary Maurice Ravel and can perhaps be traced back nearly a century to Berlioz. But French music of the early twentieth century is unthinkable without the influence of Russian music. Debussy's models were not so much earlier French composers, but the Russians Mussorgsky and Rimsky-Korsakov. His encounter with their quite different approach to harmony and orchestration in the 1880s was formative for his style. In a neat act of reciprocation, Stravinsky dedicated his *Symphonies of Wind Instruments* (1920) to the memory of Debussy, acknowledging thereby the huge influence that the Frenchman's music had exercised on his own.

It is precisely this concern with colour that fuelled the lifelong musical quest of Varèse that we have already discussed above and it is striking how composers of the postwar avant-garde, such as Pierre Boulez, have moved from the abstraction of number in total serialist works towards a music that has far more to do with colour, sonority, timbre and texture – embodied, physical aspects of musical sound. Indeed, this is perhaps the richest gain of electronic music. One of the towering figures of twentieth-century music, Olivier Messiaen, spent a lifetime thinking about musical colour even though he never worked with electronics. Colour in his music is a product of combining a rich and sophisticated harmonic system with a very particular ear for instrumental combinations. His early works owe something to the dense harmonies of Debussy and Ravel; his late works reflect the experience of a composer well aware of the achievements of electronic music. But the root of his approach to colour was highly individual; it arose from an intensely mystical expression of his religious faith (he was a devout Catholic), one often embodied in evocation of landscape and birdsong. In works like *Des canyons aux étoiles* or *Et exspecto resurrectionem mortuorum*, Messiaen fused the evocation of the divine with symbols of the natural world.

Colour in music is by no means confined to the French. There are few composers working in the latter part of the twentieth century and today for whom the tone quality of sounds is not as much part of their thinking as the notes or rhythms they use. The composer György Ligeti, for example, developed a style in the 1960s in which musical textures were built from combining many voices or instruments all performing very slightly different versions of the same line. (He called this 'micro-polyphony'.) The result, in pieces like *Atmosphères* or *Lontano* was something like the aural equivalent of watching clouds move, or seeing a study in a single colour by an abstract painter, unfold in time. In Poland, Lutosławski and Penderecki achieved very different kinds of sonorities (often violently intense in character) by a version of the same technique, whereby a group of instruments would be asked to play the same material but without coordinating precisely with each other. Both composers made use of extended techniques for producing quite new sounds from conventional instruments and often deployed thick clusters of sound. The result was highly expressionistic, even though the means seem concerned more with colour and texture. Penderecki's *Threnody to the Victims of Hiroshima* for fifty-two string instruments is perhaps the most famous example of this.

The old and the new

It is an astonishing thought that the rapturous lyricism of Richard Strauss's *Four Last Songs* is exactly contemporary with the angular modernisms of Boulez's *Second Piano Sonata*. Written in 1948, both represent a kind of extreme but one whose co-existence defines something of the plural and contradictory nature of the twentieth century. Strauss was still writing in a late-romantic idiom that was not essentially different to music from before 1900. Boulez was writing at the outer limits of what some might have considered to be music at all in 1948, an iconoclastic musical stance derived from highly theoretical considerations. But it is part of the twentieth century that a romantic musical voice persists in the face of more modern ones and the century as a whole is perhaps not well understood if we dismiss either of them. An understanding of the music of this century requires us to make sense of the fact that it includes, side by side, Strauss *and* Boulez, Rachmaninov *and* Stravinsky, Puccini *and* Schoenberg. A great many composers of the century worked away at their craft without being too disturbed by arguments about style and what constituted 'the new'. One thinks of composers like Bartók, Britten, Shostakovich, Prokofiev, Gershwin, Copland or Bernstein.

Nevertheless, the second half of the century shows a particularly bewildering array of different kinds of musical language, all of them locating themselves within the 'classical' or concert-hall tradition. At the height of the European avant-garde, a group of American composers developed a musical style known ever since as minimalism (in part, perhaps, to differentiate it from the 'maximalism' of the avant-garde). Though the movement grew out of the work of La Monte Young and Terry Riley, it is undoubtedly the success of Steve Reich and Philip Glass that has ensured the widespread and lasting influence of this music. The essence of the style is the extensive repetition of small musical figures. In the early works of these composers much of the interest of the music lay in the almost mesmeric degree of repetition underneath which the musical patterns changed imperceptibly slowly; Steve Reich's *Drumming* (1971) is a good example. Though Philip Glass has never abandoned his signature device of repeated arpeggio figures, the strictness with which musical material is constrained has been considerably relaxed in more recent works by both Reich and Glass.

Both composers attest to influences from a wide variety of sources, including non-Western music and forms of popular music, and both clearly turn their back on the kind of avant-garde music associated with the Darmstadt school. The result was that minimalism provided a kind of contemporary art music that was also genuinely popular, something reflected in the success of Glass and Reich in much bigger mediums. Philip Glass, for example, has written a number of successful operas, starting with *Einstein on the Beach*, and film scores, from *Koyaanisqatsi* (1982) onwards. This quality of popular appeal in far more public forms extends to the American composer John Adams who combines something of the minimalist reliance on repeated patterns with the kind of rich orchestral writing one more normally associates with film scores. His operas include *Nixon in China* and the *The Death of Klinghoffer*. The Dutch composer Louis Andriessen provides evidence of a wider movement of post-minimalism, in his case allying repetition with far more dissonant Stravinskian harmonies on the one hand, and materials drawn from types of popular music on the other.

A quite different group of composers working in recent decades have brought together something of the original aesthetic of minimalism with the archaic sound world and materials of pre-Renaissance music. The Estonian composer Arvo Pärt abandoned his early modernist style of the 1960s and moved towards a very simple, reduced modal musical language, marked by his aptly named work *Tabula Rasa*. Though his music is made of the repetition of very reduced materials, he has often used these in large-scale works, such as the *St John Passion* of 1982 (lasting some seventy minutes). The religious aura of Pärt's work, derived in part from the evocation of medieval choral music, is shared by the music of John Tavener. Like Pärt, his earliest compositions were in a broadly modernist idiom, but after his conversion to the Greek Orthodox church in 1977 he changed style radically. Works like *Ikon of Light* and *The Protecting Veil* exemplify his ability to create a powerful sense of ecstasy in his music, not by piling on more and more complexity, but by means of an absolute intensity of focus arising from simple materials.

In many ways, both these composers might seem to be rejecting not just the post-war avant-garde, but the whole of music history since the Renaissance. Their concern with a pre-subjective, pre-Humanist idea of music, religious in tone even when written for instruments alone, is both archaic and curiously powerful for a modern audience. Opinion is divided as to whether this represents the welcome return of a timeless spirituality or is a kind of regressive ahistoricism made possible only by ignoring history. It serves to underline how wide open music is at the start of the twenty-first century. The earnest strictures of modernism, self-conscious about its own historical position, has for some decades competed with a plethora of other musical styles – with minimalism, with film and TV music, with musical theatre, with all sorts of pop music, with world music, with the tendency of classical music to mean old music.

Postmodernism, if it means anything, suggests that we should no longer believe unproblematically in received stories – the grand narratives of history by which we justify the present by means of the past. The sheer plurality of different musical practices today is evidence enough that we live in a thoroughly postmodern world. Classical music, as we have seen, is so shaped by its history, and carries that history within it, defined through its materials, forms, instruments and ensembles as much as by less tangible ideas about what music is or does, that it occupies an odd position in a world in which history might seem to be irrelevant. Classical music is less a single kind of music and more an attitude to music or a way of thinking about it. The musicians who created the religious music of the medieval world had a very different sense of music to those who entertained at court in eighteenth-century Vienna; the composers of the twentieth-century avant-garde had little in common with the composers of Italian *opera buffa*. Classical music has always been many things, even to people of the same generation.

What it becomes next remains to be seen, but the *idea* of classical music continues to represent an astonishingly wide and rich achievement of the human imagination. At times it has embodied our sense of awe in front of the natural world, at others it has collapsed the world in comic irony. It has realized constructions of the most elegant order of which the human mind is capable, at other times it has unflinchingly sounded out the irrational depths of the unconscious. It has embodied our sense of the divine and expressed our very human desires. It has united people across boundaries of class, race and religion, at other times it has been an insidious and powerful tool for dividing people. It has reflected society as it is, and imagined it as it might be. It has embodied its hopes and played out its worst nightmares. It has recollected the past and anticipated the future. All of this it has done, while remaining 'merely' music, by diverting us from the everyday for the few minutes that it lasts, a fleeting pleasure that imprints itself upon the memory.

Further reading and suggested listening

Chapter 1
Further reading

Cook, Nicholas. *Music. A Very Short Introduction*. New York: Oxford University Press, 2000

Johnson, Julian. *Who Needs Classical Music?* New York: Oxford University Press, 2002

Kramer, Lawrence. *Why Classical Music Still Matters*. Berkeley: University of California Press, 2008

Chapter 2
Suggested listening

Byrd: *Mass for Four Voices*
Dufay: *Missa L'homme armé*; motets
Dunstable: Masses and motets
Hildegard of Bingen
Josquin: *Missa Pange lingua*; motets
Machaut: *La Messe de Nostre Dame*; chansons
Medieval Plainchant
Notre Dame school (Léonin and Pérotin)
Palestrina: *Missa Papae Marcelli*
Tallis: *Lamentations*
Taverner: *Western Wind Mass*

Further reading

Atlas, Allan W. *Renaissance Music. Music in Western Europe 1400–1600*. New York, Norton, 1998

Hoppin, Richard H. *Medieval Music*. New York, Norton, 1978

Jenkins, Lucien. *Discover Early Music*. London: Naxos Books, 2007

Knighton, Tess and Fallows, David. *Companion to Medieval and Renaissance Music*. Berkeley: University of California Press, 2009

Chapter 3

Suggested listening

J. S. Bach: Six English Suites; Brandenburg Concertos; *St Matthew Passion*

Couperin: Keyboard Music

Corelli: Concertos

Dowland: Lute Songs

Gabrieli: *Sacrae Symphoniae*

Handel: *The Messiah*; *Giulio Cesare*

Lully: *Armide*; *Cadmus and Hermione*

Marenzio: Madrigals

Monteverdi: Madrigals (Books 3–5); *Orfeo*; *L'incoronazione di Poppea*; *Vespers of the Blessed Virgin*

Morely: Madrigals

Purcell: *Dido and Aeneas*; Anthems

Rameau: *Les Indes Galantes*

Schütz: *Psalms of David*

Vivaldi: Concertos

Further reading

Hill, John Walter. *Baroque Music. Music in Western Europe 1580–1750*. New York. Norton, 2005

Perkins, Leeman L. *Music in the Age of the Renaissance*. New York: Norton, 1999

Sadie, Julie Anne. *Companion to Baroque Music*. Oxford: Oxford University Press, 1998

Schulenberg, David. *Music of the Baroque*. New York: Oxford University Press 2008

Unger-Hamilton, Clive. *Discover Music of the Baroque Era*. London: Naxos Books, 2008

Chapter 4

Suggested listening

J. C. Bach: Symphonies, Concertos and Keyboard Sonatas

C. P. E. Bach: Prussian Sonatas; Fantasias

Beethoven: Symphonies nos 1, 3, 5, 6 and 9; Piano Sonatas; 'Rasoumovsky' String Quartets Op. 59; Piano Concerto Nos 4 and 5; *Missa Solemnis*

Gluck: *Orfeo ed Euridice*

Haydn: Piano Sonatas; String quartets, Op. 33 and Op. 76; London Symphonies; *The Creation*

Mozart: Symphonies nos 39, 40, 41; Piano Concertos; *The Marriage of Figaro*; The 'Haydn' Quartets; Piano Sonatas

Further reading

Downs, Philip G. *Classical Music: Era of Haydn, Mozart and Beethoven*. New York. Norton, 1993

Johnson, Stephen. *Discover Music of the Classical Era*. London: Naxos Books, 2008

Rushton, Julian. *Classical Music: A Concise History – From Gluck to Beethoven*. London: Thames and Hudson, 1989

Chapter 5

Suggested listening

Berlioz: *Symphonie Fantastique*
Bizet: *Carmen*
Brahms: Symphonies nos 2 and 3; Piano Music
Bruckner: Symphonies nos 4, 5, 7
Chopin: Nocturnes; Mazurkas
Liszt: Symphonic Poems; *Années de Pèlerinage*
Mahler: Symphonies nos 2, 3, 5, 8
Mendelssohn: *Elijah*; *A Midsummer Night's Dream*
Mussorgsky: *Boris Godunov*
Puccini: *La Bohème*; *Tosca*; *Madame Butterfly*
Rossini: *The Barber of Seville*; *William Tell*
Schubert: Lieder; Piano Sonatas
Schumann: *Dichterliebe*
Smetana: *Vltava*
R. Strauss: *Don Juan*; *Ein Heldenleben*; *Der Rosenkavalier*
Tchaikovsky: Symphonies 4-6; Piano Concerto
Verdi: *La Traviata; Rigoletto*; *Otello*
Wagner: *Tristan und Isolde*

Further reading

McCleery, David. *Discover Music of the Romantic Era*. London: Naxos Books, 2007

Plantinga, Leon. *Romantic Music. A History of Musical Style in Nineteenth Century Europe*. New York: Norton, 1985

Whittall, Arnold. *Romantic Music. A Concise History from Schubert to Sibelius*. London: Thames and Hudson, 1990

Chapter 6
Suggested listening

Adams: *A Short Ride in a Fast Machine*
Bartók: *The Miraculous Mandarin*; Concerto for Orchestra
Berg: Piano Sonata; *Altenberg Lieder*
Berio: *Laborintus II*
Boulez: *Pli selon pli*; *Répons*
Copland: *Appalachian Spring*
Debussy: *Prélude à l'après midi d'un faune*; *La Mer*; Piano Preludes
Gershwin: *Rhapsody in Blue*
Glass: *Koyaanisqatsi*
Ives: *The Unanswered Question*; *Three Places in New England*
Ligeti: *Lontano*; Chamber Concerto
Messiaen: *Turangalîla Symphony*
Pärt: *Spiegel im Spiegel*
Poulenc: Gloria
Prokofiev: *Romeo and Juliet*
Rachmaninov: Symphonic Dances
Ravel: Piano Concerto
Reich: *The Desert Music*
Satie: *Parade*
Schoenberg: *Verklärte Nacht*; 2nd String Quartet; Variations for Orchestra
Sibelius: 5th Symphony
Shostakovich: 5th Symphony
Stravinsky: *The Rite of Spring*; *The Soldier's Tale*; Symphony of Psalms
Tavener: *The Protecting Veil*
Vaughan Williams: 5th Symphony
Webern: Symphony, Op. 21

Further reading

Griffiths, Paul. *Modern Music: A Concise History*. London: Thames and Hudson, 1994

McCleery, David. *Discover Music of the Twentieth Century*. London: Naxos Books, 2008

Morgan, Robert P. *Twentieth Century Music: A History of Musical Style in Modern Europe and America*. New York: Norton, 1991

Ross, Alex. *The Rest is Noise: Listening to the Twentieth Century*. New York: Fourth Estate, 2008

Glossary

Aleatoricism The use of chance procedures to arrive at some or all of the decisions involved in composing a piece. John Cage was the first composer to explore this idea seriously in the 1950s.

Aria A self-contained lyrical movement in an opera (or cantata or oratorio) for a solo voice (or duet). It is normally concerned with expressing a particular emotion and, in baroque music, was generally in a three-part form known as the 'da capo aria'. This has a contrasting central section followed by an ornamented return of the first section: thus, ABA.

Atonality The avoidance of any sense of key (see *Tonality*) by means of highly chromatic harmony.

Canon 1. A compositional device by which a melodic line is imitated by a second part following at a fixed distance (usually a bar or a few beats). The imitation may be at the same pitch as the original line, or at some interval higher or lower (see *Interval*). In some canons, the imitating line is also inverted (i.e. where the original goes up, the second part goes down, and so on).

2. The notional collection of 'great works' by which classical music is defined. This changes in time, as some composers and works are dropped or added in, as tastes and interests change.

Chromaticism In *diatonic* music, only the seven notes of the major or minor scale appear. Chromatic notes are those remaining notes (of the possible twelve in the Western tuning system) that are used in addition to the notes of the scale, usually for expressive effect. Thus, a 'highly chromatic' style is one that makes frequent use of these additional notes to inflect the principal notes of the scale.

Dissonance   A clash of notes that requires some resolution back to a consonant sound. Ideas of what constitutes consonance and dissonance are not so much fixed by acoustics as changeable from one period to another.

Expressionism   A movement in all the arts in Europe between about 1900 and 1925. In music, it is characterized by extreme emotions and violent disjunctions of the musical surface, as in a work like Schoenberg's *Erwartung* (1909).

Harmony   The combination of different notes heard simultaneously. Ideas have changed over time as to the principles governing both the combination of notes sounding together and how one chord moves to another.

Interval   The distance between the notes of a scale, understood as the number of scale degrees encompassed between them. The distance between the first and third notes of a scale is thus a 'third', that between the second and sixth notes is a 'fifth'.

Lieder   The term 'Lied' is German for a kind of art song (as opposed to folk song) that flourished in the nineteenth century. Its most famous practitioners were Schubert, Schumann, Brahms and Wolf.

Neoclassicism   A movement in twentieth-century music that flourished particularly in the interwar years (*c*.1920–40). It 'borrowed' materials from baroque and classical styles but treated these in an ironic manner, thus emphasizing the distance between the modern and earlier styles. Stravinsky was a key exponent, as were the French composers known as *Les Six*.

Notation   A system of signs for writing music down. In general, notation has become more complicated and detailed over the centuries.

Ornamentation   The decoration of a melodic line by the addition of extra, rapid notes in various combinations. In some cases, these are specified by the composer, in other cases they are added by the performer. The latter was understood to be part of performance practice in the baroque opera, but had died out by the end of the eighteenth century in instrumental music. It continued in Italian opera for rather longer.

Polyphony   The combination of different instrumental or vocal parts heard simultaneously. While *harmony* generally refers to the 'vertical' combination (i.e. heard at any particular moment), *polyphony* refers to the unfolding of the different parts in time (i.e. 'horizontally').

Programme music   Instrumental music that is intended, without the use of words, to represent real events, characters or places. It was an important movement in the nineteenth century, generating the symphonic poem and tone poem, which are important precursors of the musical style employed in much film music of the twentieth century.

Recitative   A kind of declamatory style developed in early opera, in which the words are delivered rapidly with only a bare harmonic accompaniment. In operas, cantatas and oratorios, recitative was often used to tell the basic story, while the musical elaboration of the ensuing emotional situations was reserved for *arias*.

Serialism   A technique developed in the 1920s by Arnold Schoenberg and his pupils for organizing atonal music. It formalized the tendency, in atonal music, to work with a recurrent set of intervals (as opposed to the more traditional idea of melody). The idea of a 'row' or 'series' of notes was taken up by the European avant-garde after 1945 and applied to other aspects of music, such as rhythm and dynamics.

Sonata   A work in several movements (usually three or four) for a single instrument with or without accompaniment (usually provided by some form of keyboard instrument).

'Sonata Form' refers to a particular structure of music used very widely for the first movements of symphonies, concertos, sonatas and chamber music works from around the middle of the eighteenth century onwards. Its importance diminished in the twentieth century. It consists of three main parts (exposition, development and recapitulation).

Thoroughbass (basso continuo)   A feature of music from *c.*1600 to *c.*1750 in which a constant bass-line, harmonized by chords (at first given in the theorbo or chittarone, later the harpsichord) provided a kind of foundation for the voices or instruments above. It was a key invention of the baroque and arose from moving away from the equality of parts in Renaissance polyphony to a focus on the upper part(s) in early baroque vocal music.

Tonality   The system of harmonic relations associated with the idea of key. Western tonality is largely defined by two kinds of scale (major and minor), which had effectively replaced the Church modes by the end of the sixteenth century. Tonality includes the idea of changing key (modulation) but is based upon the expectation of returning to the original key by the end of the piece or movement.

Verismo   A movement in opera of the later nineteenth century that sought to impart an element of realism comparable to similar ideas in contemporary literature. The works of Mascagni and Leoncavallo are often cited as examples.

Zeitopern   A movement in German opera in the 1920s and 1930s that favoured themes and settings drawn from modern life, often foregrounding modern technologies such as cars and telephones.

Index